Past Praise for the KNOWING JESUS SERIES

"In true Tara-Leigh fashion, this study is easy to follow while also challenging you to dig deeper into what the Word is saying. It's more than simply reading the Bible and answering some questions. It's a test to gauge your spiritual walk, to ask the hard questions, and to be challenged with each turn of the page about what the Holy Spirit is revealing. Whether you are a new believer or well-versed in theological teachings, this study has something to offer everyone."

Clare Thompson Sims, D-Group member

"This study delivers what D-Group has been doing for years. Instead of feeding the readers answers, it empowers them to do the work of arriving at answers through the careful study and close reading of God's Word, allowing them to take ownership of their continued growth and faith in King Jesus. What a thrilling start of a memorable new series!"

Zuzana Johansen, D-Group member

"This study helps the reader connect the Old Testament with the New by giving the perspective of the Jewish culture and customs during Jesus's day. This lens provides clarity as to why Jesus ministered and spoke as He did while interacting with both Jews and Gentiles. It also clearly communicates the relevance and life-changing power of Jesus's teachings for Christians today. It's a road map, pulling from the pages of the Old Testament and connecting it to the Gospels, pointing to our victory in Christ on the cross."

Jeremy Hall, D-Group member

"*Knowing Jesus as King* combines a deep dive into the book of Matthew with the structure of D-Group. Having been in D-Group from the very start—fifteen years ago—I can confidently say the structure creates the consistency it demands and bears much fruit for any believer. Buckle up and have faith that God will reveal Himself to you as the promised and present King over the next ten weeks."

Meghann Glenn, D-Group charter member

KNOWING
JESUS
AS SAVIOR

Also by Tara-Leigh Cobble

The Bible Recap:
A One-Year Guide to Reading and Understanding the Entire Bible

The Bible Recap Study Guide:
Daily Questions to Deepen Your Understanding of the Entire Bible

The Bible Recap Journal:
Your Daily Companion to the Entire Bible

The Bible Recap Discussion Guide:
Weekly Questions for Group Conversation on the Entire Bible

The Bible Recap Kids' Devotional:
365 Reflections and Activities for Children and Families

The God Shot:
100 Snapshots of God's Character in Scripture

Israel:
Beauty, Light, and Luxury

THE BIBLE RECAP KNOWING JESUS SERIES*

Knowing Jesus as King:
A 10-Session Study on the Gospel of Matthew

Knowing Jesus as Servant:
A 10-Session Study on the Gospel of Mark

Knowing Jesus as Savior:
A 10-Session Study on the Gospel of Luke

*General editor

THE *BIBLE RECAP* KNOWING JESUS SERIES

KNOWING JESUS AS SAVIOR

A 10-SESSION STUDY ON THE GOSPEL OF LUKE

TARA-LEIGH COBBLE,

GENERAL EDITOR

WRITTEN BY THE D-GROUP THEOLOGY & CURRICULUM TEAM

BETHANYHOUSE
a division of Baker Publishing Group
Minneapolis, Minnesota

© 2024 by Tara-Leigh Cobble

Published by Bethany House Publishers
Minneapolis, Minnesota
BethanyHouse.com

Bethany House Publishers is a division of
Baker Publishing Group, Grand Rapids, Michigan

Printed in the United States of America

ISBN 9780764243585 (paper)
ISBN 9781493446896 (ebook)

Library of Congress Cataloging-in-Publication Control Number: 2024021976

The D-Group Theology & Curriculum Team is Laura Buchelt, Emily Pickell, Meg Mitchell, Meredith Knox, Brittney Flagg, Evaline Asmah, and Tara-Leigh Cobble.

The general editor is represented by Alive Literary Agency, www.AliveLiterary.com.

Interior design by Nadine Rewa
Cover design by Dan Pitts
Author image from © Meshali Mitchell

24 25 26 27 28 29 30   7 6 5 4 3 2 1

CONTENTS

INTRODUCTION

Matthew, Mark, Luke, and John all recorded their accounts of the life of Christ. Some from firsthand experience, others from meticulous interviews of people who were there. They all bring a unique view of Jesus, and Luke's primary focus is on Jesus as the Man who came to be our Savior—the only bridge between God and humanity.

Early church tradition and other New Testament circumstantial evidence points to Luke as the author of this book. He was a close companion of the apostle Paul. Though we know very little about his conversion experience, we do know he wasn't numbered among the disciples. Luke himself tells us he interviewed eyewitnesses to Jesus's life in order to compile an "orderly account" (1:3). Though Luke's idea of order doesn't always hold to a strict respect of the timeline. He often orders his account by theme instead of chronology.

Perhaps the best evidence we have of Luke's interview process is that he tells us very specific details about the thoughts and feelings of Mary, the mother of Jesus. The only way he could have such specific information would be if he sat down and talked with her. What a fun conversation to be a fly on the wall for!

One of Paul's letters reveals that Luke was a physician (Colossians 4:14), and it's easy to see Luke's scientific approach to his writing. More than the other gospel authors, Luke pointed explicitly to Jesus's humanity and to physical details. Paul also implied that the doctor was a Gentile. If this is true, Luke is the only known Gentile author of Scripture! While Luke was well-versed in Jewish traditions, it seems he was writing to a largely Gentile audience. And though he wrote to one person, Theophilus, it appears that he expected his account to be spread far beyond just his friend.

Dr. Luke gives us something that no other gospel writer gives us—a sequel! Luke authored the book of Acts around the same time he wrote Luke. If Luke is Season 1, it would be titled "The Savior," and Season 2 (Acts) would be titled "The Church." Acts builds on all the themes of Season 1, but it answers the question "Then what happened?" Jesus defeated death at the end of Luke, but that is only the beginning. Let's dig in!

HOW TO USE THIS STUDY

While Bible study is vital to the Christian walk, a well-rounded spiritual life comes from engaging with other spiritual disciplines as well. This study is designed not only to equip you with greater knowledge and theological depth, but to help you engage in other formative practices that will create a fuller, more fulfilling relationship with Jesus. We want to see you thrive in every area of your life with God!

Content and Questions

In each of the ten weeks of this study, the teaching and questions are divided into six days, but feel free to do it all at once if that's more manageable for your schedule. If you choose to complete each week's study in one sitting (especially if that time occurs later in the study-week), keep in mind that there are aspects you will want to be mindful of each day: the daily Bible reading, Scripture memorization, and the weekly challenge. Those are best attended to throughout the week.

Daily Bible Reading

The daily Bible reading corresponds to our study. It will take an average of three minutes per day to simply read (not study) the text. If you're an auditory learner, you may prefer to listen to an audio version of these Bible chapters.

Even if you decide to do the week's content and questions in one sitting, we still encourage you to make the daily Bible reading a part of your regular daily rhythm. Establishing a habit of reading the Word every day will help fortify your faith and create greater connections with God.

If you decide to break the study up into the six allotted days each week, your daily Bible reading will align with your study. Days 1–5 will follow our study of Luke, Day 6 features a psalm that corresponds to our reading, and Day 7 serves as a catch-up day in case you fall behind.

Scripture Memorization

Memorizing Scripture isn't busywork! It's an important part of hiding God's Word in our hearts (Psalm 119:11). Our passage—Luke 1:46–55—is known as Mary's Magnificat, the poem/song she wrote in celebration of the fact that the Savior was coming into the world. We encourage you to practice it cumulatively—that is, *add* to what you're practicing each week instead of *replacing* it. We quote the English Standard Version (and some of our resources are in that translation as well), but feel free to memorize it in whatever translation you prefer. We suggest working on each week's verse(s) throughout the week, not just at the last minute. We've provided some free tools to help you with this, including a weekly verse song: MyDGroup.org/Resources/Luke.

Weekly Challenge

This is our practical response to what we've learned each week. We want to be "doers of the word, and not hearers only" (James 1:22). You'll find a variety of challenges, and we encourage you to lean into them all—especially the ones you find *most* challenging! This will help strengthen your spiritual muscles and encourage you in your faith. As with the memory verse, you'll want to begin this practice earlier in the week, especially because some weekly challenges include things to do each day of the week (e.g., prayers, journaling, etc.).

Resources

This is a Scripture-heavy study, and you'll find yourself looking up passages often. If you're new to studying Scripture, this will be a great way to dig in and sharpen your skills! You will feel more equipped and less intimidated as you move through each chapter. Some questions may ask you to refer to a Bible dictionary, commentary, or Greek or Hebrew lexicon, but you don't need to purchase those tools. There are lots of free options available online. We've linked to some of our favorite tools—plus additional resources such as podcasts, articles, and apps—at MyDGroup .org/Resources/Luke.

Groups

Because each week has a lot of questions in the content, we offer the following recommendation for those who plan to discuss the study in a weekly group meeting. As each member is doing their homework, we suggest they mark their favorite items with a star and mark any confusing items with a question mark. This serves as preparation for the group discussion and helps direct the conversation in beneficial ways.

┌─ Scripture to Memorize ─┐

Mary said, "My soul magni-
fies the Lord."

Luke 1:46

Luke 1–2:

The Arrival of the Savior

Note: If you haven't yet read "How to Use This Study" on pages 11–13, please do that before continuing. It will provide you with a proper framework and helpful tools.

DAILY BIBLE READING

Day 1: Luke 1:1–25

Day 2: Luke 1:26–56

Day 3: Luke 1:57–80

Day 4: Luke 2:1–21

Day 5: Luke 2:22–52

Day 6: Psalm 16

Day 7: Catch-Up Day

Corresponds to Days 274–275 of *The Bible Recap*.

WEEKLY CHALLENGE

See page 41 for more information.

Luke 1:1–25

 **READ LUKE 1:1–25**

1. **Review 1:1–4.**

Luke's investigative eye for detail is immediately evident in the first twenty-five verses of his gospel. He assured his friend Theophilus that the research had been done, the eyewitnesses had been interviewed, and the evidence was clear. The letter he was about to write was not fable or fantasy—it was biography. The story of the Savior is true.

2. **Review 1:5–7.** Think of this as Zechariah's and Elizabeth's "about pages," or Luke's description of their social media profiles. Write down as many details about Zechariah's and Elizabeth's lives as possible.

In first-century Israel, it was believed barrenness was evidence of divine disfavor, and Zechariah and Elizabeth had likely been waiting for a child for nearly fifty years. Friends probably suspected them of some secret sin. Barrenness was also an acceptable grounds for divorce. Zechariah could've legally freed himself from Elizabeth and their barren situation. Some scholars believe they had even moved outside of town to avoid daily public shame. But God looked on them with no such shame, affirming that they both stood "righteous before God" (v. 6).

God had never left Zechariah and Elizabeth, and they hadn't left Him either. Their faithfulness wasn't determined by what God had *not* done for them. As people who had grown up in the homes of priests, perhaps the psalms of their youth still rang in their ears, "My eyes will be on the faithful in the land" (Psalm 101:6 NIV). Perhaps God's wait was not God's no. He is always on time, forever omnisciently punctual.

3. What are you waiting for God to do? Following Zechariah's and Elizabeth's examples, spend some time with God, asking Him again. Write out a short prayer below.

4. **Review 1:8–10. Look up a diagram of the first-century Jerusalem temple.** Take a quick temple tour, making special note of where priests would've burned incense. (See Exodus 30:7–8.)

Only priests from a specific lineage could serve in the temple (1 Chronicles 23–24). And from the origination of the temple until Zechariah's time, the number of priests serving in the temple had greatly increased (there were approximately 20,000 in Jesus's time). The custom of the day was to cast lots to see who would assist with the offerings and speak a blessing of praise and thanksgiving to God. A priest may only get one chance in his entire lifetime. Considering this, imagine the expectation rising in Zechariah as he entered the temple to do his service and speak his blessing. What a privilege. What a moment.

5. **Review 1:11–17.** What did the angel say would be true of their son, John the Baptist (we'll call him by his initials, JTB, for short)?

6. **Revisit 1:15, then read Numbers 6:1–21.** How would JTB fulfill the Nazirite vow?

Throughout Scripture, God calls His people to a holy practice of consecration. To consecrate something means to set it aside for special and holy service to the Lord. Both people and objects can be consecrated. Though these consecrated things were just common people and everyday objects, they were to be handled differently.

Think back to the "temple tour" diagram. There was bread used for everyday use, then there was "shewbread." There were lampstands for sale on marketplace streets, and there were lampstands set aside for the Holy Place alone. There was oil used by Jewish mothers to make dinner for their families, and there was oil used to anoint priests to enter God's holy presence. The same items—but they held varying degrees of importance depending on their purposes. The greater the proximity to the presence of God, the greater the level of consecration. Holy things get handled differently.

JTB was to be the one to prepare the way of the Lord—the long-promised Messiah, the Savior of the world. This level of proximity and height of purpose required greater consecration. What an honor God had appointed him for!

7. What "normal" aspects of your life may God be inviting you to start handling differently? Is there anything you feel called to consecrate—to set apart for holy use?

8. **Read Malachi 4:5–6.** What does this Old Testament prophecy reveal about JTB's calling?

9. **Review Luke 1:18–23.**

The word *angel* means "messenger," and they aren't deceased humans. They're a unique type of being God created that can exist in both the spiritual and physical realms to do one of their jobs, which is to transmit messages from the spiritual realm to the physical realm. Only four angels are named in scripture, and we see one of them in today's reading. Gabriel has the special assignment of foretelling the birth of JTB to a long-barren couple. Imagine being the bearer of good news from a holy God to a longing man, only to be met with hesitation!

10. Is it hard for you to believe God might be generous to you in an area where your longings are unfulfilled? Why or why not?

As a result of Zechariah's unbelief, Gabriel said he would be mute until JTB's birth. Some scholars believe this caused him to miss his one opportunity to speak the blessing of praise and thanksgiving in the temple. It seems there may have been an abrupt end to his one special day of service. Nevertheless, God blessed Zechariah and Elizabeth with the child He promised through the angel.

11. **Review 1:24–25. Now read it in the NLT.**

12. Spend some time writing down evidence of God's kindness to you. Let your praise erupt with Elizabeth's.

Luke 1:26–56

READ LUKE 1:26–56

Notice the details in this passage—the time, the people, the descriptions. Luke's account is always helping us place real people in real time. Before Mary was in the lineage of our faith history, she was just a girl living in Galilee getting ready for a wedding.

1. **Review 1:26–33.**

It may be easy to casually read over this familiar encounter, but these verses hold great significance! There are roughly four hundred prophecies about the Messiah in the Old Testament. The people of Israel had waited for the fulfillment of these prophecies for thousands of years, quoted them around Passover tables, whispered them in prayers, shared them as a means of encouragement. And in these eight verses, the prophecies began their fulfillment in a town of little significance to a young girl with no pedigree or polish. This moment was a piercing and poignant declaration of eternal significance breaking through four hundred years of silence. It began a cataclysmic shift in human history.

2. It's important for every believer to grow in their knowledge of the New Testament fulfillment of Old Testament prophecies. Look up the

prophecies below and fill in the table. Use a commentary or study tool if it's helpful.

Old Testament prophecy	Who wrote it?	How did Jesus Christ fulfill it?
Genesis 3:15		
Isaiah 7:14		
Psalm 22:16–18		

3. **Review 1:34–35, then look back at 1:18–20.** Compare and contrast Zechariah's and Mary's questions.

Zechariah and Mary seemed to ask similar questions, but they received very different responses. Why was Zechariah made mute while Mary received a clear answer? In short, "man looks on the outward appearance, but the LORD looks on the heart" (1 Samuel 16:7). God welcomes our questions. He delights in us seeking understanding. But there is a heart that asks out of childlike desperation, and there is a heart that demands answers out of pain, arrogance, or entitlement. God muted Zechariah not because He loved him less, but likely to align his faith again. Hope deferred can certainly wear deep ruts of discouragement. Sometimes only silence can fill up the furrows of doubt worn by years of waiting.

4. What is one of the biggest questions you're currently asking God? Ask the Holy Spirit to reveal whether it is being asked in childlike faith or entitlement. Sit in silence for a moment and wait for His voice. Write down anything that comes to mind. Remember that it's His kindness that leads us to repentance (Romans 2:4).

5. **Review 1:36–38.** What does it mean that "nothing will be impossible with God"?

To rightly apply Scripture to our everyday lives, it's vital that we always return to the context. Though this declaration should deeply encourage every reader, it's not meant to be used as an amen on every petition, however well-meaning it may be. This passage is indeed *for* us, but it is not *about* us. It's about Christ! It's a type of celestial amen. The long-awaited Savior was coming; the wait was over. And He was coming in a way few expected Him—lowly, quietly, through the womb of a humble woman. Truly, nothing will be impossible for God. Let that truth be fully anchored in Christ alone.

6. Review 1:39–45. Now reread the declarations about JTB in 1:14–17. What is being revealed about JTB's calling in these two passages?

Elizabeth, elderly and pregnant, was carrying the fulfillment of many years of waiting in her womb. And yet, this long-awaited blessing of a baby *leapt* in the presence of the unborn Jesus. Already, JTB was fulfilling his calling, jumping in utero as if to testify to his mother, "Here is the *real* one you've been waiting for—the true fulfillment of your every longing." How quickly did Elizabeth turn to Mary and tell her how blessed she was above all women, including herself! She was truly blessed with JTB, but her greatest blessing had just arrived in the person of Christ.

And so, filled with the Holy Spirit, Elizabeth got to be the first human to herald Christ as the Messiah! God truly does more than we could ask or imagine. By the way, it's worth noting that Luke often highlighted and affirmed the role of women in the gospel story. He pointed to these details more than any other gospel writer.

7. Review 1:46–55. How many times did Mary say "me" or "my"? How many times did she say "He," "Him," or "His"?

Here we have Mary's psalmist moment (and our memory passage for this study). In the presence of such an outpouring of the Holy Spirit, and as she housed the Holy One Himself, she couldn't help but to pour out a song of praise. Over and over, Scripture affirms that this is all about Christ. Elizabeth was a woman of faith, JTB held an incredible calling, and Mary was worthy of high honor. But only Christ is the main character.

Luke 1:57–80

† READ LUKE 1:57-80

Our Scripture today builds like the crescendo in a great song. Soon, we'll be at the birth of Jesus. Luke was writing in this spirit of expectation as he recounted JTB's birth—neighbors rejoicing, Zechariah's mouth opened, a beautiful chorus of praise leading us into Bethlehem.

1. **Review 1:57–58, along with 1:13–14.**

After years of waiting, the time had finally come for Elizabeth to give birth. Imagine the joy and expectation surrounding this elderly couple as they welcomed their baby son. This is a beautiful picture that preaches an even more beautiful message: *Our blessings are not just for us*. God allowed Elizabeth and Zechariah to receive the blessing of a son, but that blessing was prophesied to be a source of joy, for "many will rejoice at his birth" (v. 14). And rejoice they did! This child who would point many to the way of ultimate joy was fulfilling his destiny before he could even speak a word.

2. **Look up *covenant* in a Bible dictionary.** Write down the definition.

3. **Review 1:59–60.**

4. **Read Genesis 17:1–14.** How did God link circumcision to covenant? Why was JTB's name important?

This scene gathered around JTB's family may be unfamiliar—or even uncomfortable—to us. But this was a monumental day for all Jewish families. It was a celebration that connected them to each other, to the generations previous and following, and to God Himself. The act of circumcision was more than a ritual or rite of passage—it was a sign of the binding agreement God made between Himself and His people. God intentionally connected circumcision and covenant.

In the covenant's inauguration in Genesis 17, God blessed Abram's generational family, spoke of a new life in a new land, and gave him a new name—Abraham. The ceremony of circumcision was the commemoration of a new family, a new life, a new name. Is it any wonder that Scripture would mark this specific moment with a massive conversation around what JTB's name should be? It would be through his mission that he would call people to awareness of a covenantal shift. The Savior was coming, and He would bring a new covenant—one that would institute a new family, a new life, and a new name through the shedding of His blood.

5. **Review 1:61–66.** What act caused Zechariah to be able to speak again? What was the first thing he did when he could speak?

The silence did the good work it was meant to do in Zechariah's heart. He didn't use the discipline of God as an opportunity for bitterness, but saw it as a sign of God's loving correction. When questioned about the baby's name, he responded in simple yet devout obedience, "His name is John." It was obedience that opened his mouth, and praise was the overflow.

6. Zechariah's obedience was simple, yet visible. Fill in the table below to help yourself practice this posture of obedience with him.

What simple act of obedience is God calling you to?*	Give yourself a deadline.	Who do you need to share this with as a means of accountability?

*Think small here. For example: Start a budget, read my Bible every day this week, memorize Scripture, etc.

7. **Review 1:67–80.** Draw what you think a "horn of salvation" looks like.

As soon as Zechariah was able to speak, he immediately began praising God and prophesying about Jesus. He didn't talk about his son or his gratitude for his mouth being opened—he rejoiced in Christ as Savior. Some scholars believe these first words he spoke were the blessing he was originally supposed to offer months earlier on his day of service in the temple. Held back in a divine cliffhanger through his temporary muteness, these words weren't silenced or stifled—they steeped in his soul until they erupted, all the more potent and praise-filled, from his softened heart and opened mouth.

Horn of salvation probably isn't a phrase you use in everyday language, but the imagery is powerful. The salvation Christ brings is a *glorious* one because it is "raised up" above and beyond any other form of redemption, political savior, or radical revolutionary. And it's a *bountiful* salvation, overflowing like the most beautiful Thanksgiving cornucopia ("horn of plenty") you've ever seen. It overflows with the bread of life, living water, sustenance and satisfaction that can come by no other means. And it's a *powerful* salvation—just as the strength of many animals is in their horns, so the strength of God's people is in their Savior. There's no power that can overcome or overwhelm the name of Jesus. Anything that would stand to confront Him will fail.

Zechariah's final prophecy joined with the voices of all the prophets who had come before him, calling us to look again at this high and lifted-up horn of salvation, Jesus Christ. As John Trapp wrote in his commentary on Luke, "There were many Prophets, yet had they all but one mouth: so sweet is their harmony."* And it is this harmony that will carry us to the birth of the Savior Himself.

---

* John Trapp, *A Commentary or Exposition Upon the Gospel according to Saint Luke* (Ann Arbor: Text Creation Partnership), chap. 1, p. 48, https://quod.lib.umich.edu/e/eebo/A63067 .0001.001/1:7?rgn=div1;view=fulltext.

Luke 2:1–21

READ LUKE 2:1–21

Heads up: This day might ruin a lot of your Christmas nostalgia. Luke's careful attention to detail invites us to put a new spin on a familiar phrase: Don't miss the *trees* for the *forest*. Sometimes we can visit a place so often that we forget to actually look at it. The colors become faded, the images get blurred, the true and miraculous details of the story are lost in familiar fable.

1. **Review 2:1–5.** Slow down and notice the "trees." Fill in the chart below with the details you find.

Who commanded a registration be taken?	
Who was meant to respond to this registration?	
Where were they to go?	
What was the main point of an ancient "census"? (This may require a quick internet search.)	
What region was Joseph in when the decree went out?	
What town?	
What region was he to travel to?	
What town?	

What is the walking distance between those two towns? (This may require a quick internet search.)	
What was mentioned about Joseph's lineage that may be important?	

It's important to slow down and put in a little work to set ourselves in the right time and place. Caesar Augustus was the first emperor of the Roman Empire. Before this, Rome had always been a republic, ruled by groups and laws. One man reigned as the Augustus—the "sacred" and "exalted" one. He had set himself up as a political savior, the one to finally calm a war-wrought Mediterranean basin. The humble Savior was about to be born under the reign of a self-elevated one. He would not come in pomp and circumstance, but in poverty and squalor.

2. **Review 2:6–7.** Luke gives us four important facts that reveal the setting of Jesus's birth. Let's zoom in on these and make sure the picture in our minds matches the details on the page. **Using a commentary or Bible dictionary, look up "swaddling cloths."** Write down what you find.

In those days, the status of a family was indicated by the splendor and costliness of their birth cloths. Children of wealthy parents would be wrapped with white linen or purple cloth, fastened with a brooch. Jesus had no such clothing. The word translated *swaddling cloths* comes from a Greek word meaning "to tear." Picture Mary and Joseph scrambling for scraps and wrapping their divine Son in whatever was lying around. Far from home, they made do with little. This is evidence of Jesus's family being poor, and it's one of many proofs that the Savior came for the lowly and the displaced.

Mary "laid Him in a manger, because there was no place for them in the inn." A manger is a feeding trough for animals, but most were chiseled from stone. Trees were in short supply in ancient Israel, but stone abounded.

This scene likely took place in a cave—the kind of place many people kept their animals during the winter—and the feeding troughs were often carved right into the cave walls. But because the animals were in the fields with the shepherds (2:8), the cave would've likely been empty of animals, leaving a space for Mary and Joseph (and possibly other visitors in town for the census) to lodge.

And right there, in that unassuming, probably filthy place, the Savior was born. Imagine the smell. Imagine the commotion. And imagine the cry of heaven's hero piercing through it all.

Speaking of smells, let's talk about shepherds.

3. **Review 2:8–14.** Fill in the chart below based on 2:10.

What did the angel bring?	Of what?	For whom?

In first-century Israel, shepherds were often females—and sometimes males, especially if there were no female children in the family—of poor reputation. As a group, they held a pretty low status in society. Even though some of them were entrusted with the birthing, protecting, and raising of the temple flock for ritual sacrifices, they were generally viewed as unreliable outcasts. And yet the angel entrusted this good news to them. A great joy for all people indeed.

4. The angel said the shepherds would recognize the Savior because He'd be "wrapped in swaddling cloths and lying in a manger." How would these two details reveal the Savior's identity to the shepherds? **Use a Bible study tool for help.**

Ceremonially, when a perfect lamb was born, it was set aside as a sacrifice, and it had to be wrapped in "swaddling cloth" as a means of protection, warmth, and preservation. Only a perfect lamb could be used as a sacrifice. These shepherds would've wrapped a young lamb in cloth numerous times, knowing that it was just being preserved until it could be sacrificed. The clue the angel was giving them was not only so they could recognize the child's identity, but so they could recognize the child's purpose. This human baby would be a sacrificial lamb, sent to be the Savior of mankind. What better group to first tell about this good news of great joy? He had come! And He would give Himself up as the perfect sacrifice for our salvation.

5. **Review 2:15–21.**

The night ended with the shepherds running to tell the good news. Mary, on the other hand, "treasured up all these things . . . in her heart." When it comes to the good news God shares with us, there are times for telling and there are times for treasuring. The shepherds ran to tell. Mary paused to treasure. Both are necessary in this life of following Jesus. It's in the telling that we draw others close to Him, and it's in the treasuring that we draw closer to Him ourselves.

6. What is one good thing you learned from today's reading that you can tell someone today? What is one good thing you heard from God today that you need to treasure and keep for yourself?

Luke 2:22–52

 **READ LUKE 2:22–52**

Most of today's reading is centered around the temple. So if you didn't get a good temple tour before, you'll be well acquainted after today!

1. **Review 2:23–24, then read Matthew 5:17 and Leviticus 12.**

Jesus came to fulfill every aspect of the law, even in His infancy. So His family took Him to the temple to present Him to the Lord. Mary also walked in obedience to Levitical law, bringing two birds as a sacrifice. Birds were the sacrifices of the poor (Leviticus 12:8). Mary and Joseph may not have been able to afford a lamb, but God entrusted them to carry the perfect lamb of God, the One who would be sacrificed for the salvation of all.

2. **Review 2:25–35.** What had Simeon heard from the Lord? Why was this so important?

There had been four hundred years of silence between the Old and New Testaments. But Simeon served as proof that God hadn't been completely silent; He was still speaking to individuals who were walking in righteousness.

3. Something (or someone) shows up for the first time in 2:32. Circle what you think the answer is.

"...a light for revelation to the Gentiles, and for glory to your people Israel."

Look at the temple diagram. Draw a line around the Court of Women. Mark every point of entry to the temple with an X.

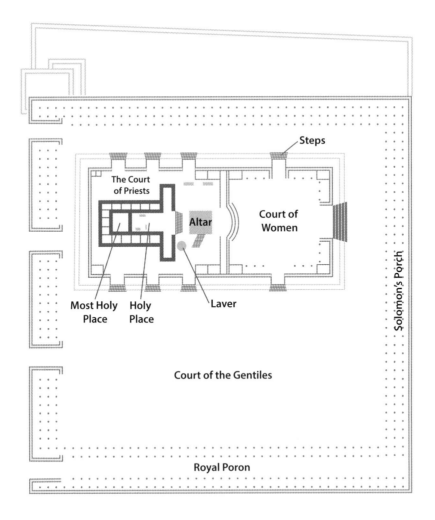

Every line and every X reveals a barrier between the Gentiles and the presence of God. It's remarkable (and revealing) that in the designs for His temple, God included a space for the Gentiles at all. Centuries earlier, this architectural detail served as a hint of the good news to come—but Israel hadn't grasped it yet. Jews had always drawn clear lines of delineation between themselves and Gentiles in every aspect of life. They were a people set apart, after all. God's chosen people—Gentiles not included.

Now, here stood Simeon, where Gentiles weren't allowed to go, declaring a word no one expected: "Salvation has come for the Jew *and* the Gentile." No longer would there be a line of separation. Both are brought close, and the two are made one. Imagine if anyone in the temple overheard this!

Apparently, someone did.

4. **Review 2:36–40.**

5. What title does Scripture give Anna? Why is this significant?

The fact that Anna is mentioned by name shows God's honor of women yet again. We don't know how Anna got her title, but we know she walked with the Lord, "worshiping . . . night and day." One can only hope she was still there praying when Jesus returned twelve years later.

6. **Review 2:41–45.**

7. Mary and Joseph went to the Feast of Passover to celebrate their people's miraculous rescue from Egyptian slavery (Exodus 12). **Read Deuteronomy 16:16.** How many times a year were faithful Jews to go to Jerusalem for ritual feasts?

Mary, Joseph, and Jesus would've been traveling to and from Jerusalem with a large crowd from Galilee. You've probably been on a big friend or family trip like this before. Now, take away any minivans, car seats, and truck stops, and it makes sense that a kid could get away from you.

After a day's downhill journey, Mary and Joseph realized Jesus was not, in fact, among their crew. They likely set out early the next morning to make the uphill climb back to Jerusalem.

8. **Review 2:46–52.**

9. Where did they find Jesus? What was He doing?

Mary and Joseph finally found Jesus after three days. He was seated in the temple "among the teachers" and asking questions. This became a familiar mark of Jesus's teaching strategy for the rest of His earthly ministry—

asking questions He already knew the answers to, inviting further dialogue. In the four Gospels, Jesus was asked 183 questions. In contrast, He *asked* 307 questions. He only ever answered three directly.

Why? His goal isn't to frustrate or confuse us, because God isn't a God of confusion (1 Corinthians 14:33). He asks questions to draw us closer, to open our understanding. Questions are an invitation to further dialogue. Further dialogue requires more time. More time leads to more time spent *together*. More time spent together leads to relationship and understanding. And that's what Jesus wants.

10. Take some time to engage with these questioning conversations below.

Scripture	What questions were asked of Jesus?	What questions did Jesus ask in return?	What was the result?
Luke 2:48–51			
Matthew 22:15–22			
Mark 11:27–33			

11. **Compare 2:51–52 to Hebrews 4:15–16.** What similarities do you notice?

Jesus, full of power, still left the temple to be submissive to His earthly parents. Jesus, full of wisdom, still grew up and increased in understanding. Jesus *chose* to bind Himself to the human condition. He *chose* to be with us so that we could be with Him. And what a gift—because He's where the joy is!

12. What stood out to you most in this week's study? Why?

13. What did you learn or relearn about God and His character this week?

Corresponding Psalm & Prayer

 **READ PSALM 16**

1. What correlation do you see between Psalm 16 and this week's study of Jesus as Savior?

2. What portions of this psalm stand out to you most?

3. Close by praying this prayer aloud:

Father,
   "You are my Lord; I have no good apart from you" (Psalm 16:2). I praise You because You are my Creator, Sustainer, and Fulfiller. You

made me, You keep me safe, and You give me joy! You sent Your Son to fulfill Your covenant and offer Your joy.

I confess that I'm an unworthy recipient of Your goodness. I forget the miracle of Your Son's birth, and I doubt You as the One who performs miracles. You have shown me the path of life in its fullness, but I've chosen my own way. I've run after idols instead of You. Forgive me, God.

Will You make me Your content servant? Help me notice like David that because of You—"the lines have fallen for me in pleasant places; indeed, I have a beautiful inheritance" (Psalm 16:6). And help me proclaim like Mary, "I am the servant of the Lord; let it be to me according to your word" (Luke 1:38).

I surrender my life to You, Lord—every moment of my day, each decision I make, I yield my will and way to Your perfect will and way.

I love You too. Amen.

Rest, Catch Up, or Dig Deeper

✝ WEEKLY CHALLENGE

The two chapters of Luke from this week's study are filled with eruptions of praise: Elizabeth when Mary visits, Mary and her Magnificat, Zechariah and his prophecy, Simeon's rejoicing, Anna's praise. Using your journal, write your own poem or song of praise, thanking God for who He is and what He has done. If it's helpful, use Mary's Magnificat as a guide. If you're not creative, don't worry—it doesn't have to rhyme! Or if you especially enjoy creative pursuits, feel free to make an art piece using your poem.

Luke 3–5:
The Power of the Savior

DAILY BIBLE READING

Day 1. Luke 3

Day 2. Luke 4:1–15

Day 3. Luke 4:16–44

Day 4. Luke 5:1–16

Day 5. Luke 5:17–39

Day 6. Psalm 32

Day 7. Catch-Up Day

Corresponds to Days 277–278 of *The Bible Recap*.

WEEKLY CHALLENGE

See page 72 for more information.

Luke 3

 **READ LUKE 3**

1. **Review 3:1–6.**

Luke's precise record-keeping opens our second week of study. His account of the political leaders at the time of JTB's ministry is confirmed by multiple non-biblical historical sources. In modern-day America, Luke's list would be similar to naming the president of the country, the governor of a state, and the mayor of a city. And yet, even with powerful leaders exercising an iron-fisted rule, an unruly prophet from the wilderness upstaged them all.

After the word of God came to JTB in the wilderness, he began his work. Four hundred years of silence had passed since God had last sent a prophet to speak to His people. And the time had come not only for another prophet, but the forerunner of the Messiah.

2. **Read Malachi 3:1.** What did the final Old Testament prophet tell the people to expect?

JTB prepared the way for the Messiah, preaching and baptizing. He proclaimed the need for repentance: turning away from sin and toward God. Baptism itself doesn't secure God's forgiveness, but it does signify our "repentance for the forgiveness of sins" (Luke 3:3).

Malachi referred to JTB as a "messenger of the covenant" (Malachi 3:1). In the Old Testament, God established a covenant with His people that set them apart for a special relationship with Him. Through Jesus, the new covenant not only redeems Israel, but extends that redemption to believers from all nations. Ethnicity is an inheritance. Faith in Jesus is a decision.

3. Review 3:7–14.

4. In the table below, write each question asked and who asked it.

Verse	Questioners	Question Asked
3:10		
3:12		
3:14		

5. Why do you think Luke recorded three distinct groups of people asking the same question?

JTB didn't tell any of the groups to quit their day jobs and commit their lives to full-time ministry. He instructed them to provide for others generously, to do their work uprightly, and to live their lives faithfully. The beautifully inclusive good news of forgiveness invites everyone, even tax collectors, to join in. And the rightly specific requirement of that forgiveness is repentance. Generosity and integrity aren't required for salvation, but they serve as evidence of a genuinely changed heart.

6. If you asked JTB "What then shall we do?" with your work in mind, how do you think he would answer?

7. **Review 3:15–20.**

JTB told his listeners some harsh truths, speaking about vipers, wrath, an axe, a winnowing fork, and fires, but Luke said JTB "preached good news to the people" (v. 18).

8. What was the good news JTB preached? Why does that news matter for you today?

Like He did with the Old Testament prophets, God sent JTB to deliver a message to His people. But unlike that of the Old Testament prophets, the message JTB was sent to deliver was that the Messiah *had come*. Theirs was the message of "When?" and his was the message of "Now!" And this message was the final straw on King Herod's list of so-called offenses JTB had committed, so he had JTB arrested and imprisoned.

9. **Review 3:21–22.**

Jesus didn't begin His ministry by going to meet with the political leaders or even the high priests. He went to the desert and submitted Himself to baptism. Some faith traditions believe His baptism purified the waters for future generations of Christians, while others believe He was setting an example for future Christians to follow. But both views agree on this: Jesus didn't need to be baptized as a symbol of repentance, because He certainly didn't need to repent. And yet His flawless adherence to His mission was marked by God the Father's approval: "You are my beloved Son; with you I am well pleased" (v. 22).

10. **Review 3:23–38.**

Matthew's gospel opens with the genealogy of Jesus, but in Luke's gospel, the genealogy marks the beginning of Jesus's ministry. You may notice that there are also a few differences between the lists of ancestors given in these two gospels.

11. Review 3:38 and read Matthew 1:2. Who is the oldest ancestor listed in each genealogy?

Matthew, a Jew, traced Jesus's lineage back to the father of the Jewish people. Luke, a Gentile, traced Jesus's lineage back to the father of mankind. Both are true. Jesus is a descendant of Abraham, through whom "all peoples on earth" (Genesis 12:3 NIV) will be blessed. And Jesus is a descendant of Adam, from whom we've all descended. Jesus is the Messiah God's people were promised, and He's the Savior all people can know.

12. What do these two genealogies reveal about the heart of God?

Luke 4:1–15

READ LUKE 4:1–15

Today's reading opens with Jesus in the wilderness for forty days. Forty is a significant number throughout Scripture. During their forty years in the wilderness, the Israelites faced three major temptations, which are similar to the temptations our Savior faced in the wilderness. The apostle John summarized these types of temptations in 1 John 2:16.*

1. **Read 1 John 2:16.** What are the three temptations of the world?

2. **Review 4:1–13.**

*Nick Batzig, "How Does Jesus' Temptation Link Him to Israel?" *Tabletalk*, January 22, 2020, https://tabletalkmagazine.com/posts/how-does-jesus-temptation/.

For forty days, Jesus was "being tempted by the devil" (v. 2). Though we don't know what the specific temptations were, the language here implies He was being tempted *the entire time*. Then, at the end of that period, the enemy made a last-ditch effort to make the Savior of the world sin—and he used Scripture to do it.

3. What Old Testament Scripture did the enemy twist to tempt Jesus (4:10–11)? **Use a study Bible for help.**

Jesus answered the devil's intentionally misinterpreted Scripture with its true meaning. Twisting Scripture to suit one's own selfish purposes is an old and dangerous game. Assuming the meaning of Scripture based on an out-of-context verse often leads to disappointment and pain. And those who deceive others with disinformation will be held to account (Galatians 1:9). Studying the Bible—learning how all of God's Word works together—protects us from believing these lies ourselves and stops us from deceiving others with them.

4. What Scriptures have you heard twisted—either intentionally or unintentionally? How did you recognize they were being twisted?

5. Can you think of a time when you believed a twisted Scripture and it affected you negatively? If so, briefly describe its impact.

The temptations Jesus and the Israelites faced are universal. These temptations have existed since the fall. In Genesis, the serpent tempted Eve's pride by twisting God's words, and she believed him and gave in to sin. Adam was likewise tempted and followed her into sin.

6. **Review 3:21–22 and read Genesis 3:17–19.** Contrast what God the Father said to Adam with what God the Father said about Jesus.

Passage	What did God say?
Genesis 3:17–19	
Luke 3:21–22	

7. **Read Romans 5:18–19.** How is Jesus the true and better Adam?

Jesus—fully man—was tempted just as Adam was, just as the Israelites were, and just as we are. But Jesus—also fully God—did not sin. Satan takes the good gift of God's Word and twists it into prideful, harmful sound bites. Since the beginning of time, humankind has been deceived by this trick. But Luke reminds us that there is hope, not in ourselves, but in the One who has never been deceived. Jesus's victory over the enemy here is clear and points us forward to His ultimate victory over sin and death.

8. **Review 4:14–15.**

So far, at four major events in Jesus's life recorded in this gospel, Luke has referenced the power of the Holy Spirit.

9. Review the verses below, then match each reference to the Spirit with the corresponding event in Jesus's life.

Scripture	Event
1:35	Jesus's baptism
3:22	Jesus's temptation
4:1	The start of Jesus's ministry
4:14	Jesus's conception

10. Why is the presence of the Spirit vital in these events?

The presence of the Holy Spirit brings power. His power showed up when a virgin conceived, a dove descended, and temptation was overcome. And at the right time—with that sustaining power of the Spirit—Jesus's ministry began.

11. How have you seen the power of the Spirit at work in your life? Be specific.

DAY 3

Luke 4:16–44

⊤ READ LUKE 4:16–44

At the very beginning of the world, God established the seventh day—the Sabbath—as a day of rest. The fourth commandment affirms not only its value, but its necessity and holiness.

1. **Review 4:16–19.**

As a law-abiding Jew, Jesus spent His Sabbath in the synagogue. At the time, a common practice was for local synagogues to invite visiting rabbis—teachers—to read Scripture on the Sabbath. The rabbi would read the text and then spend time explaining it. Synagogue attendees were accustomed to lengthy interpretations of the law and the prophets. But Jesus did something entirely different.

2. According to 4:18–19 and Isaiah 61:1–2, what did Jesus come to do?

After reading aloud the prophecy about Himself, Jesus didn't immediately offer further explanation. Instead, He rolled the scroll back up, gave it to the synagogue attendant, and *sat down*. Everyone stared at Jesus. Were they silent with confusion? Did they whisper to each other in anticipation? Were they anxious? Excited? Then Jesus spoke again. He said only a few words, but those words represented a shift in the world as they knew it.

3. **Review 4:20–22.**

4. Summarize what Jesus told the people in the synagogue in 4:21. How did they respond?

5. **Review 4:23–27.**

The people had heard about the miracles and healings in Capernaum, and Jesus knew they wanted the same things for themselves. Maybe they wanted Him to prove His divinity, or maybe they just wanted His miracles, but Jesus knew they still wouldn't accept Him. So He reminded them that when God's prophets Elijah and Elisha were rejected by Israel, God sent those prophets elsewhere with the message. Jesus was telling His own people in His own hometown that He hadn't come only for them, but for the Gentiles as well.

6. **Review 4:28–30.**

7. Fill in the table below to contrast the crowd's two responses in this brief period of time.

Passage	The Crowd's Response
4:22	
4:28–29	

8. Why do you think the two responses were so different?

Jesus spoke of the expansion of His kingdom to include the Gentiles, whom the Jews hated. There were times throughout their history when God forbade them from interacting with Gentiles. After years of slavery and exile and oppression, they were a self-preserving people. Yet Jesus—their long-awaited Messiah—was telling them He came as the Savior for the *whole world.*

Before we point fingers at the Jews for rejecting God's plan, we need to examine our own hearts. When we are confronted with truth that contradicts our own traditions or self-preserving beliefs, our reactions are often closer to that of the people of Nazareth than we'd care to admit. Especially when that truth challenges us to love those we'd rather avoid or ignore.

9. Is there a truth you've learned about God that corrected one of your misconceptions? Describe how you felt when you came to realize the truth.

10. **Review 4:31–37.**

Sometime after Jesus's miraculous escape (that even Dr. Luke doesn't attempt to explain) from His hometown mob, He was teaching in a synagogue in Capernaum on another Sabbath. When first-century rabbis read the texts in the synagogue, they often explained those texts to the people by quoting other rabbis' opinions. But Jesus taught using another tactic.

11. According to 4:32, what was different about Jesus's teaching? Why?

Jesus was interrupted by a man with the spirit of an unclean demon. When the demon spoke Jesus's name and identity, Jesus rebuked him and cast the demon out. A short while later, Jesus repeated this same instruction to more demons, forbidding them from speaking.

12. Why do you think Jesus didn't allow the demons to speak, even when they spoke the truth about who He was?

This is the first example in Luke of what's known as the messianic secret, where Jesus wanted to wait to reveal His full identity until the time was right, telling people and even demons to keep quiet.

On the same Sabbath, after teaching in the synagogue, Jesus went to the house of Simon (also called Peter and Simon Peter), one of His first disciples. Simon Peter's mother-in-law was sick with a high fever, and the family was worried about her.

Jesus healed her so completely that she didn't even need recovery time. She immediately got up and served them. Her response was right, and it reminds us that when we truly understand what God has done for us, we'll praise Him and we'll serve Him.

Once the sun set, the Sabbath was over, and the work that was prohibited during the Sabbath daylight resumed. Crowds of people carried their sick loved ones to Jesus. Jesus was fully human, and He'd had a long day filled with teachings, demons, and healings—He was probably tired. He could have healed the entire crowd at once. But He didn't.

13. **Review 4:38–41.**

14. What did Jesus do in 4:40? How has He paid individual attention to you?

15. **Review 4:42–44.**

As the sun rose, Jesus was finally able to retreat, but the people still tried to follow Him. They wanted Him to stay, but He refused. God's perfect plan to share the good news of the kingdom must be fulfilled.

Luke 5:1–16

READ LUKE 5:1–16

As each gospel writer told the good news of Jesus through his unique lens, some recurring events were recorded in different orders.

1. Write the transitional phrases at the beginning of each of the following verses:

- 5:1—"on one occasion"

- 5:12—

- 5:17—

2. How do these phrases reveal that the events in Luke aren't necessarily in chronological order?

3. **Review 5:1–11.**

Luke first recorded the beginning of Jesus's ministry, then he established Jesus's lordship over the disciples. That's where we begin today. The area around the Lake of Gennesaret, also known as the Sea of Galilee, was home to expert fishermen like Simon Peter, James, and John. They'd spent their lives learning the profession of their fathers, but this particular night, they'd caught nothing. Washing their nets after their exhausting failure, Simon Peter consented to Jesus's request to use his boat to teach the crowd, and he pushed it farther back from shore. After teaching, Jesus told Simon Peter to take his boat out and let his nets down one more time.

4. How did Simon Peter respond to Jesus in 5:5–7? What happened?

A once-in-a-lifetime catch—one that any fisherman would have spent the rest of his life bragging about—filled two boats so full that they began to sink. But Simon Peter didn't pay attention to the fish.

5. What did Simon Peter do in 5:8? What did he say? Fill in the chart below.

Action	Words

Here, Simon Peter was only beginning to understand who Jesus is. As Jesus's ministry continued, God gave Simon Peter a deeper understanding of Jesus's divinity, which Simon Peter only fully understood after Jesus's death and resurrection. But with the first glimpse of the power and kindness of his Savior, Simon Peter's response was to rightly feel his own insignificance in comparison with Jesus's magnificence.

6. Describe a time when you were struck by your own smallness in light of Jesus's glory.

When God gives us a genuine recognition of who we are and who He is, our only right option is obedience. Jesus even told Simon Peter what the result of his obedience would be: "From now on you will be catching men" (v. 10).

Jesus called His first three disciples and told Simon Peter that from that point forward, they would fish for men (from the Greek word *anthropos*, which means both men and women). These young disciples couldn't have fully understood what this meant, but they knew that anything with Jesus was better than everything without Him. So they left it all—their family, their property, and the still-flopping, net-breaking catch of a lifetime—to follow their Savior.

7. Have you, or someone you know, been called to leave something behind to follow Christ? What was it?

8. **Review 5:12–16.**

Some left everything they had to follow Jesus. Others begged Him with all the strength they had left to heal them. In the Bible, "leprosy" could mean any number of severe skin diseases. The man who came to Jesus was "full of leprosy," meaning his was an advanced case of whatever form of leprosy he had. With some forms, over time, the skin became so severely infected that extremities would rot or even fall off. In compliance with Jewish law, and to prevent the spread of disease, someone with leprosy was sent away from the rest of the community. This suffering, isolated man saw Jesus and begged for healing.

9. **Read 5:13 below.** Underline what Jesus said. Circle what He did.

Jesus stretched out his hand and touched him, saying, "I will; be clean."

Jesus could have healed this lonely, desperate man with a word, but He didn't. Jesus not only came close to the man, but *touched* Him.

Jesus sent the healed man to the priest so he could fully return to participation in his community, but He told the man to "tell no one." This is another instance of the messianic secret, which we learned about in Day 3 of this week (see page 58).

10. Keeping in mind what happened with the crowd in Nazareth in Luke 4, why do you think Jesus told the man not to tell anyone who healed him?

Despite Jesus's instructions to stay silent, word about Him spread, and crowds came. They heard His teaching and asked for His healing. And Luke made note that throughout that time, Jesus "would withdraw to desolate places and pray" (v. 16).

11. Why do you think Luke included Jesus's habit of withdrawing to pray? What does this mean for your life?

Luke 5:17–39

READ LUKE 5:17-39

Today we met the Pharisees, who were Jewish religious leaders in Jesus's time. Pharisees were very concerned with keeping the law, so they took God's laws and built a broader fence around them to keep people from accidentally breaking the law. What may have started as a well-intentioned attempt to interpret God's law with precision and clarity turned into a legalistic hunt to shame anyone who walked past the man-made fences. Here's an illustration of how this worked: If the speed limit was sixty miles per hour, the Pharisees would "draw the fence" at fifty miles per hour, just to make sure that no one with a broken speedometer got anywhere close to driving over the speed limit. Then they began to treat their fences as though they were actually the law itself, giving speeding tickets to anyone who drove fifty-five miles per hour.

1. **Review 5:17–26.**

It was in this climate that a group of friends brought a paralytic man to Jesus. They'd heard about His miracles and were so determined to get their friend to Him that they moved roof tiles to do it. Jesus saw their faith and acted. But He didn't just heal their friend.

2. Why was it easier for Jesus to say "your sins are forgiven"?

The book of Daniel prophesied that the Son of Man—Jesus—would reign eternally. In 5:24, Luke introduced the title "Son of Man" to show Christ as the Savior who forgives sins. Old Testament prophets told God's people what their Savior would do, and He was finally here. In 5:21–24, Luke shows Jesus's divinity in three ways: He heals, He perceives thoughts, and He forgives sins.

3. **Read each prophecy below.** Match it with the example of its fulfill-ment from this event.

Scripture	Event
Isaiah 35:5–6	He forgives sin
Isaiah 66:18	He perceives thoughts
Micah 7:18	He heals

4. **Review 5:27–32.**

Later, Jesus saw the tax collector Levi, who was almost certainly the man we know as Matthew the gospel writer. Tax collectors in Jesus's time were considered traitors by their fellow Jews. They worked for the Roman empire, taking money from their own people to fund the very army that oppressed them. Levi was working in his tax booth, gathering funds to support Rome, but Jesus had different plans for him.

5. Fill in the chart below according to 5:27–28.

Jesus's Words	Levi's Actions

When Levi hosted a feast for Jesus and invited some of the religious rulers of the area—the Pharisees—they were appalled at the presence of sinners around the table. What the Pharisees refused to see was that they were sinners too.

Like the Pharisees, it can be easy for some Christians to err on the side of legalism, avoiding interaction with "tax collectors and sinners" altogether. We may insulate ourselves to avoid corruption (or at least the appearance of it). Other Christians take Jesus's righteous example here and push it to licentiousness. We may insist that we can spend our time anywhere we want, in the company of anyone we want, without it damaging our faith or our obedience. Stepping too far on either side of the road—legalism or licentiousness—makes us fall off the path of following Jesus.

6. **Look up the various definitions of the word *licentious* in two different dictionaries.** Describe it using your own words.

Jesus ate with sinners. He welcomed them. He called them. And because of His perfect love, they left His presence radically changed. They didn't make Jesus unclean; on the contrary, He made them clean.

7. **Read 5:32 below.** Circle who Jesus called. Underline what He called them to.

> "I have not come to call the righteous but sinners to repentance."

Jesus's mission was better than legalism and it was better than licentiousness. Our calling is better than legalism and it's better than licentiousness.

8. How has legalism hindered your walk with Jesus? How has licentiousness?

9. **Review 5:33–39.**

The dinner guests asked Jesus why His disciples didn't fast. To answer them, Jesus asked them a question in return and told them a couple of parables. Parables are short teaching stories with unnamed characters. They are usually meant to illustrate one main point, so they aren't intended to be picked apart or overanalyzed.

In His answer, Jesus neither affirmed nor denied the value of fasting—though He fasted Himself—but pointed out that fasting comes from a posture of grief, uncertainty, or repentance.

10. How is rote, uninspired fasting like putting a new patch on old clothes? **If needed, use a study Bible or a commentary for help.**

Then Jesus told them a different, but related, parable. An old wineskin is brittle and inflexible, but new wine needs room to breathe and expand. Remember the Pharisees' insistence on their own interpretations of God's law? They'd become so rigid that they couldn't hold the joy, love, and beauty Jesus offered.

While 5:39 may seem confusing, Jesus didn't reverse His meaning here. He was criticizing the Pharisees for clutching their old wine tightly, insisting that it was good—better than the new wine. The old wine *was* good. But Jesus was offering them new wine that was infinitely better. And by refusing to taste and see for themselves, they robbed themselves of the richest, boldest, most perfect wine ever poured. He's better than anything we're stubbornly clinging to, and He's where the joy is!

11. What stood out to you most in this week's study? Why?

12. What did you learn or relearn about God and His character this week?

Corresponding Psalm & Prayer

READ PSALM 32

1. What correlation do you see between Psalm 32 and this week's study of Jesus as Savior?

2. What portions of this psalm stand out to you most?

3. Close by praying this prayer aloud:

Father,
    I praise You for Your steadfast love! In Your great mercy, You invite me to confess my sin to You. You forgive my sin and give me

joy, surrounding me with Your steadfast love. I'm blessed because of You!

You've instructed me and taught me the way to go, but at times, I've been a licentious sinner who insists Your grace allows me to sin more. And at other times, I've been a legalistic Pharisee who credits my salvation to my own self-righteousness. All the while, I've twisted Your holy Word to defend my sin. Forgive my many transgressions. Cover my sin by the blood of Your Son, Jesus.

May I be so overwhelmed by Your power and kindness that I—like Simon Peter—fall on my face in worship. Like the crowds listening to JTB, remind me to ask, "What then shall I do?" Prepare and equip me for whatever call You place on my life. Make me willing to leave it all behind, abandoning temporary comfort for glorious eternal life with You!

I surrender my life to You, Lord—every moment of my day, each decision I make, I yield my will and way to Your perfect will and way.

I love You too. Amen.

Rest, Catch Up, or Dig Deeper

† WEEKLY CHALLENGE

In Luke 4, Jesus responded to the enemy's misuse of Scripture with its correct use. According to the list of the "armor of God" in Ephesians 6:10–18, every piece of armor—except for one—is for defense. The only piece of armor used for offense is "the sword of the Spirit, which is the word of God." This week, take some time to practice wielding your sword. Make a list of at least five verses that have helped you in times of temptation (or search for them if you don't know some offhand). You can either write the list down and post it in your home or keep it as a note on your phone—anywhere that gives you quick access to it. Aim to read through the list aloud at least once daily this week.

Luke 6–7:
The Kingdom Agenda of the Savior

Scripture to Memorize

"For He has looked on the humble estate of his servant. For behold, from now on all generations will call me blessed."

Luke 1:48

DAILY BIBLE READING

Day 1. Luke 6:1–19

Day 2. Luke 6:20–36

Day 3. Luke 6:37–49

Day 4. Luke 7:1–17

Day 5. Luke 7:18–50

Day 6. Psalm 40

Day 7. Catch-Up Day

Corresponds to Days 282 and 284 of *The Bible Recap*.

WEEKLY CHALLENGE

See page 100 for more information.

Luke 6:1–19

READ LUKE 6:1–19

As readers far removed from the cultures and practices of first-century Israel, our first section of the week might feel a little strange. To understand the context, we need to take a quick glimpse into the fourth commandment given to Moses in the law.

1. **Read Deuteronomy 5:12–15.** What did God forbid on the Sabbath? Why?

2. **Review Luke 6:1–5.**

In the approximately 1,500 years between Moses and Jesus, the rabbis wanted to make sure the law was honored, so they set boundaries—or "built fences"—around the laws, as we discussed in Week 2. While the

Sabbath law itself was broad, the religious leaders created their own very specific, detailed list of what was prohibited on the Sabbath. This was known as the oral law, in contrast to God's written law. Eventually, these rules were treated as if they were God's laws, not the opinions of man. According to the Pharisees in Jesus's day, picking and eating a handful of grain constituted work, which gave them grounds to accuse His disciples of breaking the Sabbath.

3. The Pharisees overemphasized a strict adherence to the fourth commandment. How might this have been a stumbling block to their ability to recognize Jesus as the long-awaited Savior?

When the Pharisees accused Him of sinning, Jesus, who is Lord of the Sabbath, made a not-so-subtle dig back at them. These men prided themselves on their knowledge of the Scriptures, so it was an affront to their learning when Jesus asked them, "Have you not read what David did?" *Of course they had.* Jesus's example from the life of David (1 Samuel 21:1–6) demonstrated how "the Sabbath was made for man, not man for the Sabbath" (Mark 2:27). Even though Jesus had used Scripture to prove that human need supersedes religious ritual, the Pharisees continued to cling to their rules.

4. When you grow in your knowledge of God's Word, how does it impact you? Does it tend to puff you up? Does it humble you and transform your heart? What's the difference?

5. **Review 6:6–11.** How did the Pharisees miss the point of the Sabbath? What laws did they break while trying to prove themselves right?

It's important to note that Jesus wasn't trying to abolish laws or downplay the Sabbath, but to clarify its purpose. God gave His people the Sabbath as a means of flourishing, but the religious leaders had turned it into oppressive limitations. Imagine being so hard-hearted that witnessing a miracle hardens your heart even more!

6. **Review 6:12–13.**

Jesus didn't just follow rules; He was totally submitted to the Father and dependent on the power of the Spirit. On the day before a critical ministry moment, Jesus went alone to the mountain and prayed through the night until sunrise.

7. **Using a Bible dictionary, look up the definitions of *disciple* and *apostle*.** How are they similar? How are they different?

Though there were many who followed Jesus, the number of those who were committed to daily life with Him was much smaller.

8. **Review 6:14–16.**

9. Select one apostle you know little about and do some research. Write down what you find. What does it reveal about the heart of God that He chose that person as an apostle?

Jesus didn't make mistakes. Each one of those twelve men was chosen for a purpose—even Judas. These were the chosen few who passed along the message of our Savior, which carried on from generation to generation, all the way to us.

10. **Review 6:17–19.**

The last few verses in today's reading briefly skimmed over what was likely a chaotic scene. Jesus, who led His twelve by example, took them along in ministry, right into the great multitude of people—including the sick, troubled, and demonized.

11. Look at the map below. How far had people traveled to get to where Jesus was ministering (near Capernaum)?

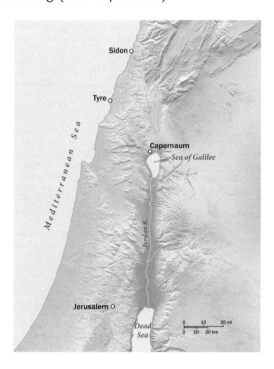

12. Why did the crowds come to see Jesus?

13. What drives you to get near Jesus?

Luke 6:20–36

✝ READ LUKE 6:20-36

A great multitude was not only trying to get near Jesus, but trying to get their hands on Him to access His power for healing.

1. **Review 6:20–23.**

In the midst of this melee, Jesus looked up at His recently chosen twelve and began teaching. If we're wise, we'll listen carefully to Jesus's words because He was beginning what functionally served as a three-point TED Talk that could be titled "The Agenda of the Kingdom." Some scholars believe this was the same message Matthew recounted in the Sermon on the Mount (Matthew 5–7). Others think Jesus used the same content at another time. Either way, when Scripture repeats content, it's worth paying closer attention.

2. **Using a concordance, write down the definition for the word** *blessed* **in the Greek.** How is it the same as your understanding of the word? How is it different?

Point number one in Jesus's kingdom agenda deals with earthly positions versus kingdom positions. While the Jewish people *were* looking for a savior, they wanted one who would give them temporal salvation in the form of political or material blessings. What Jesus outlined must've caught them completely off guard, because what He was talking about wasn't just the temporal, but also the eternal.

3. Fill in the chart below. **Use a commentary as needed.**

Blessed are the . . .	Human perspective of why they're not blessed	Spiritual value of the human circumstance
Poor	They cannot provide for themselves and must look to others for their provision.	
Hungry		
Weeping		Being broken hearted over sin and its effects allows us to value the joy that comes from the presence of the Lord and His perfection.
Hated / Excluded / Reviled / Spurned		

This list feels backward, but it confronts us with the spiritual reality. As broken and fallen humans, we approach the kingdom in a far worse position than simply neutral; we approach it with an insurmountable debt. By taking on the mantle of Savior, Jesus made it possible for us to be a part of His upside-down kingdom—where indebted sinners are not only forgiven, but granted rewards in heaven!

4. **Review 6:24–26.** Write out the parallels between 6:20–23 and 6:24–26. How can having earthly abundance be an obstacle to God's kingdom?

We tend to think of "woes" as threats, but what's found in the nuance of the Greek word οὐαί is an exclamation "of grief or of denunciation."* It's almost as if Jesus is saying, "Heavyhearted, I warn you that if you depend on human blessing as your hope, that's the only blessing you'll experience. You'll be eternally cut off from the true blessings of the kingdom." Jesus wasn't saying it's wrong to have material abundance; He was warning that putting your hope and identity in that material abundance leads to eternal disaster.

5. **Review 6:27–31.**

Jesus continued with point two in His "The Agenda of the Kingdom" message. This point emphasized the character of those who are kingdom-minded. It may be an easy point to comprehend, but it's virtually impossible to obey apart from the power of the Holy Spirit.

* "G3759—ouai—Strong's Greek Lexicon (KJV)," Blue Letter Bible, accessed 13 May, 2024, https://www.blueletterbible.org/lexicon/g3759/kjv/tr/0-1.

6. **Using a concordance or a Greek lexicon, look up the word *love* from 6:27.** Circle the kind of love Jesus was talking about. Why do you think Jesus used this particular form of *love* here?

Eros: Romantic love

Storge: Familial / brotherly love

Philia: Friendship love

Agape: Sacrificial / active love

If we were to ask, "What is the character of the kingdom?" the answer would be *love*. But Jesus didn't leave that answer as an abstract, intangible one; He gave three specific examples of how to live out agape love in the kingdom of God.

7. In 6:27–28, what are the three ways Jesus said to live out the action of loving our enemies with agape? Why are each of these so difficult?

8. In an effort to put Jesus's words into practice, pause and pray specifically and intentionally for the person whom you least want to pray for.

It's important to note that Jesus's commands to pray for those who abuse you and turn the other cheek do not condone abuse, nor does He suggest that someone must remain in a place where abuse is happening. Jesus was outlining the heart posture and character of a kingdom-minded person when they find themselves in these situations.

9. From 6:29–30, write out a modern-day example of each of these culturally specific scenarios. **Use a commentary if it's helpful.**

The only way to be at peace with someone insulting you, stealing from you, or ripping you off is to have the kingdom mindset that God will defend you and that He can be trusted to provide exactly what you need.

10. **Review 6:32–36.**

Jesus used the Socratic method (asking questions that had obvious answers) to reinforce why the character of the kingdom is vital. In a death-blow to our entitlement, He said to expect nothing in return for our good behavior. But then, in a shocking reversal, He said God is preparing a reward for those who live out this agape love. The Father has rewards in store for us that far exceed what the world offers!

11. Fill in the blanks from 6:35.

He is _____ to the _____ and the _____.

12. What does this reveal about God's heart? Describe a time when you experienced this kindness personally.

13. Write 6:36 below.

14. How does the Father's mercy equip and enable you to live out agape love toward others, even your enemies?

Luke 6:37–49

✝ READ LUKE 6:37-49

Yesterday's reading finished with Jesus in the middle of His talk about the kingdom's agenda. His first point dealt with earthly positions versus kingdom positions, and His second point revealed that agape love defines the character of a kingdom-minded person.

1. **Review 6:37–38.** Why do you think Jesus linked judgment and generosity? What lessons could be learned from this pairing?

Many people cite 6:37 as an excuse to do whatever they want without accountability. However, Scripture consistently points to the value of discernment, presenting it as vital. Loving people with agape love isn't the same as offering blanket approval to all their actions.

2. **Review 6:31 and 6:38b and summarize the instructions.** How well do you live out this kind of agape love? On a scale of 1–10, rate yourself in this area.

3. **Review 6:39–42.** Fill in the chart below.

Passage	Spiritual Parallel	Kingdom Character Application
6:39–40		
6:41–42		

When Scripture talks about physical sight, it almost always has a deeper layer of meaning that refers to a spiritual ability to understand the kingdom perspective. Here, Jesus pointed out that loving someone with agape love is also multilayered: It means walking in humility with careful judgment and intentional generosity. He encouraged His disciples to use spiritual eyes when deciding whom to follow.

He also emphasized the individual responsibility for self-reflection and personal growth as a means of loving others well. It's always easier to see someone else's sins than our own, but Jesus told His disciples that confronting someone else's small issue while refusing to acknowledge our own significant issue isn't consistent with agape love. Instead of both things being ignored, both things should be addressed.

4. What negative impact could come from handling these verses poorly? What positive impact could come from handling these verses well?

5. **Review 6:43–45.**

Before moving on to His final point, Jesus emphasized that the character of a person would always be revealed by what came out of their mouth. Jesus told His audience that each tree would be known by its own fruit.

6. When you think of the "fruit" in your life, what encourages you? What convicts you?

Jesus's third point in his kingdom agenda message addresses entrance into that kingdom.

7. **Review 6:46–49.** What is the danger of wanting Jesus to be our Savior but not our Lord?

8. What were the benefits, drawbacks, and rewards of each builder's approach?

	Benefits	Drawbacks	Rewards
Builder #1			
Builder #2			

As always, Jesus didn't give this analogy in a vacuum, but in the context of the kingdom agenda. Though it may feel backward at times, entrance to the kingdom through Jesus the Savior is what allows us to live on firm footing, even when the storms come. Nowhere in Jesus's explanation of the agenda of the kingdom does He say its citizens will be spared from trials, abuses, or storms—in fact, He assures us we'll face them.

9. What are some practical ways we can determine the foundation of our lives?

Building something requires our time, energy, emotion, and resources, and it reveals what we value. Though the world may offer quicker comforts and measurable treasures, their worth is temporary and rapidly depleting. But kingdom citizens have nothing to fear when the streams break and the flood waters of life rise. They will be safely standing on the firm foundation of our Savior—Jesus Christ—experiencing *and* expressing agape love.

Luke 7:1–17

 **READ LUKE 7:1-17**

1. **Review 7:1–10.**

With His talk on the kingdom agenda finished, Jesus went back home to Capernaum, where He was met with requests for His attention. But this request came from an unlikely source—a Roman centurion. He had sent elders from among the Jews to make this appeal to Jesus.

2. **Do a web search for "first-century Roman centurion" and write down a few things you find interesting about the role.**

The man seeking Jesus's help was a high-ranking Gentile soldier, a leader in the army that oppressed Israel. He was asking Jesus for healing, but not for himself—his request was for his servant. Roman masters had every right (and it was generally expected) to kill a servant who fell ill and was no longer able to serve. The centurion's desire to seek help for his servant and to seek that help *from Jesus* reveals something bigger was happening in his heart. His actions displayed both his compassion and a humble willingness to break from societal norms.

3. Using the ESV, fill in the blanks in the verses below:

7:4—"He is _____ to have you do this for him . . ."

7:6—"Lord, do not trouble yourself, for I am ____ _____ to have you come under my roof."

The elders effectively served as professional references for the centurion, praising him for demonstrating a love for Israel and their God. They lauded him as worthy, but only moments later, the centurion denounced his own so-called worthiness, proclaiming the value of Jesus instead.

4. **Look up 7:6 in a concordance or lexicon.** What is the definition of the word *Lord* in this context? What does it say about the man's view of Jesus in the context of his request?

5. **Read Matthew 28:18.** What authority does Jesus have?

6. **Read John 5:30.** Whose authority is Jesus under?

Luke tells us that Jesus not only healed the servant, but marveled at the insights this Roman centurion had into the kingdom. While God's chosen people should've had faith and expectation in the coming Savior, it was this unnamed Gentile, a tool of Rome's oppression, who had more faith than the Jews. While this statement would've almost certainly caused outrage among Jesus's Jewish audience, it serves as additional confirmation that He came to be the Savior of *all*.

7. **Review 7:11–17.** How far was the journey from Capernaum to Nain by foot? Do a web search for help.

Jesus and His followers made their grueling uphill journey southwest to the city of Nain, and even before he could enter the town gate, He encountered an opportunity for ministry. A funeral procession was taking place, and mourners were carrying a man to his final resting place.

8. What does 7:12 reveal about the deceased? Given this information, what might the future have held for his mother? **Use a commentary for help.**

When Luke referred to Jesus as Lord in 7:13, he used the absolute form of the word, emphasizing His deity* and authority over the situation. The Savior saw this woman, who had a miserable road ahead, and He had compassion on her. If He were unable to change this woman's situation, then telling her not to weep would've been cruel. But Jesus knew what was about to happen.

* C. Marvin Pate, *Luke: Moody Gospel Commentary* (Chicago, Illinois: Moody Publishers, 1995), quoted in D. Guzik, "Study Guide for Luke 7," Blue Letter Bible, https://www.blueletter bible.org/comm/guzik_david/study-guide/luke/luke-7.cfm.

9. Just as Jesus saw the grieving woman, the Lord sees us. Describe a time when it comforted you to know the Savior saw you in your pain.

Jesus approached the dead man, touched the open coffin, and spoke directly to him as if he were alive. His contact with the dead typically would've made Him ceremonially unclean according to Levitical law, but death wasn't transmitted—*life* was! Dr. Luke didn't miss the chance to emphasize one last time that the man had been dead before telling us he sat up and began to speak. When Jesus gave him back to his no-longer-grieving mother, the people glorified God.

10. According to 7:16–17, what five things happened as a result of this miracle?

1.

2.

3.

4.

5.

During His ministry, Jesus didn't raise every dead person He came across, so to expect this every time would be foolish. But what we can expect is that because Jesus is the Savior, everyone who believes in Him will experience something even greater: a spiritual resurrection to an eternal kingdom in His presence!

Luke 7:18–50

READ LUKE 7:18-50

Just as Jesus had disciples who learned from Him, so did His cousin, JTB. Not long before this, Herod imprisoned JTB for a few "offenses," including preaching the gospel (3:18–20) and boldly stating that Herod shouldn't have married Herodias because she was already married to his brother (Matthew 14:3–4).

1. **Review 7:18–23.**

From his prison cell, JTB dispatched his disciples to ask Jesus an important question.

2. Why do you think JTB sent his disciples to ask this question? What did they witness when they arrived?

JTB didn't seem to be doubting that Jesus was the promised Savior, but in the face of certain death, he seemed to want the affirmation that there was more than what he was enduring. Jesus didn't just answer with a yes—He gave examples from His ministry to serve as proof. Then He told them to tell JTB what was happening physically, spiritually, and prophetically.

3. Match the miracle with the Old Testament prophecies about the Savior. (Some verses will be used more than once.)

Event	Scripture
The blind receive sight	Isaiah 26:19
The lame walk	Isaiah 35:5
The deaf hear	Isaiah 35:6
The dead are raised up	Isaiah 61:1
The good news is preached to the poor	

Jesus finished His answer to JTB by adding, "Blessed is the one who is not offended by me" (v. 23). Some scholars believe this was Jesus's way of sending JTB a message that he would not be freed from prison. In fact, the second half of Isaiah 61:1 references liberty for the captives and prophesies about opened prison cells—but Jesus didn't include that part in His reply. And JTB certainly would've noticed its absence from the well-known prophecy of the Messiah. While Jesus *was* the long-awaited Savior, JTB's freedom from his prison cell wasn't part of the plan.

Much like they had gathered to hear Jesus, these same crowds had gathered to hear JTB. As we've seen, JTB was a prophetic forerunner to Jesus, prophesied by Malachi (3:1). But Jesus says he was more than a prophet. He was the only prophet in Scripture who ever got to see the Savior face-to-face!

4. **Review 7:24–30.** Using your favorite Bible commentary, describe what Jesus meant by saying that JTB was the greatest yet the least in the kingdom.

On Day 3 of Week 1, we looked at Luke 1:59 and talked about covenants. And here, in this passage about JTB, Jesus drew a clear line between the old and new covenants. While JTB was the greatest when it came to the earthly realm, his earthly status paled in comparison to the blessings of kingdom life under the new covenant (1 Corinthians 11:25, 2 Corinthians 3:6, Hebrews 8:6–13)!

JTB's baptism was one of repentance. Those who had recognized their spiritual need and were baptized were far more likely to grasp this concept from Jesus. But those who rejected their need to repent had a much more difficult time recognizing their spiritual poverty.

5. How does personal repentance prevent a heart from growing hard and critical toward others? Is repentance part of your regular rhythm as a follower of Christ? Why or why not?

6. **Review 7:31–35.**

Jesus explained a hard reality. If someone's heart is bent toward criticism, they will find something to criticize regardless of the truth. A critical spirit is evidence of an unrepentant heart.

7. Review 7:36–40.

We know many of the Pharisees rejected Jesus outright, but here we see that some seemed authentically interested in His message, namely Simon. While we aren't told Simon's motivation for inviting Jesus to a dinner party, we know that Jesus rarely spent His time teaching the hard-hearted.

8. Using your favorite commentary, describe a few of the astounding things about the series of events in 7:37–38. What must the woman have recognized about Jesus?

9. Using the table below, imagine what Simon might have been thinking in 7:39–40.

About himself	About the woman	About Jesus

10. **Review 7:41–50.** What is the kingdom perspective behind the practical example Jesus gave in 7:41–43? How is it relevant to your life?

Jesus had the kingdom perspective in mind when He asked Simon, "Do you see this woman?" It seems Jesus meant for Simon not only to see the woman standing there, but what her actions said about her heart. The word He used here carries the implication of beholding, discerning, perceiving. It seems He didn't just want Simon to *look at* her but to *see* her.

This woman recognized her spiritual poverty and worshiped the only one who could do anything about it. Because of this, her sins were forgiven. Jesus once again displayed His deity and gave the woman a new identity. Likewise, when we recognize our spiritual poverty and come to Jesus in repentance and worship, we are granted forgiveness of our sins too. And like this woman, we're able to go in peace, knowing that He's where the joy is.

11. What stood out to you most in this week's study? Why?

12. What did you learn or relearn about God and His character this week?

Corresponding Psalm & Prayer

 **READ PSALM 40**

1. What correlation do you see between Psalm 40 and this week's study of Jesus as Savior?

2. What portions of this psalm stand out to you most?

3. Close by praying this prayer aloud:

Father,
   You make my steps secure, and You put a song of praise in my mouth. Even if I spent every word I had left proclaiming Your won-

drous deeds, I wouldn't be able to name them all. I rejoice in Your goodness!

And because of Your goodness and mercy, I don't just acknowledge my sin; I agree with You about it. There is a log in my eye that needs to be removed.

I've been quick to be critical. I've labeled Your image bearers as my enemies, and I've hated them. I've been dismissive of my own sin while judging my brothers and sisters harshly for theirs. I've ignored the Sabbath—which You gave as a gift for flourishing—because I don't trust You to provide. I've put my identity in my wealth—or lack of it—because I chose to forget what You've done for me and how You promise to always provide.

Help me not to forget what You've done. Whether I face opposing armies in battle, like David, or judgmental critics, like the apostles, help me. Like You've done before, I ask that You do it again.

I surrender my life to You, Lord—every moment of my day, each decision I make, I yield my will and way to Your perfect will and way.

I love You too. Amen.

Rest, Catch Up, or Dig Deeper

⊤ WEEKLY CHALLENGE

This week's challenge comes from our Day 5 study. Martin Luther said, "When our Lord and Teacher Jesus Christ said, 'Repent, etc.,' he meant that the entire life of believers be a life of repentance."* Confession and repentance are often linked. They aren't merely the acts of acknowledging our sin. Confession is agreeing with God about our sin, and repentance is turning away from our sin.

The New Testament authors spill a lot of ink on both topics, yet these practices rarely show up in the lives of many Christians today. Scripture calls us to confess our sins to God (1 John 1:9), and to others as well (James 5:16). And the consistent message of Jesus throughout His ministry was to not just confess, but repent—to agree and to turn away.

Every day this week, practice the disciplines of confession and repentance—even if the sin is something as seemingly "small" as your attitude in traffic, your jealousy over someone else's possessions, or your joking gossip behind a friend's back. Either set a daily reminder to confess or—better yet—do it in the moment. Choose another Christian to confess your sin to each day, ask them to pray for you that you will turn away from the sin, then lean into the beautiful promises God offers you in conjunction with your obedience: "Confess your sins to one another and pray for one another, that you may be healed" (James 5:16). "If we confess our sins, he is faithful and just to forgive us our sins and to cleanse us from all unrighteousness" (1 John 1:9).

* Martin Luther, *The Ninety-Five Theses and Other Writings*, trans. and ed. William R. Russell (New York: Penguin Books, 2017), 3.

Luke 8–9:

Motives Matter to the Savior

DAILY BIBLE READING

Day 1. Luke 8:1–25

Day 2. Luke 8:26–56

Day 3. Luke 9:1–17

Day 4. Luke 9:18–36

Day 5. Luke 9:37–62

Day 6. Psalm 127

Day 7. Catch-Up Day

Corresponds to Days 287 and 290 of *The Bible Recap*.

WEEKLY CHALLENGE

See page 126 for more information.

Luke 8:1–25

 **READ LUKE 8:1-25**

Today opens with Jesus and His followers on the move again.

1. **Review 8:1–3.**

The first two verses in this section might be easy to gloss over, but Luke identified that some of the people in Jesus's caravan were women. In ancient Israel, this likely would've been unheard of. The fact that these women were acknowledged and that some of them were also *named* is worth noting. Mary and Joanna were from very different backgrounds. Joanna, from Herod's household, likely had money and status, while Mary was a former social pariah who had seven demons before Jesus cast them out.

2. Based on what you know about ancient Near Eastern culture (or do a web search for help), why is it noteworthy that Jesus included (and Luke mentioned) the women who traveled with Him? What does that reveal about the heart of God?

Jesus's ministry demonstrates that He values people of all stripes—no matter their background, wealth, wounds, or position in society. Perhaps that's one reason such large crowds were drawn to Him. In front of one of these crowds, Jesus taught a parable about seeds and the different types of soil a seed might encounter.

3. **Review 8:4–15.**

In this agrarian society, He would've been speaking a language familiar to most, but the point of His lesson wasn't clear. The disciples pulled Him aside and asked Him to explain. It can sometimes feel like Jesus's teachings are hard to comprehend, but even His closest students often had to ask for clarification! Jesus told His disciples that this was intentional. Only "those who have ears" would hear the message. He concealed the main point of His message to demonstrate the uniqueness of those who seek further. He made the parable just hard enough to expose the crowd's hardness of heart.

The disciples, on the other hand, showed they understood who Jesus was, and they were determined yet humble enough to ask questions when they didn't understand. Jesus rewarded them for their heart posture and explained the parable.

4. When was the last time you didn't understand something in Scripture? Did you seek to understand? What does this reveal about how you view God?

In this parable of the four soils, only one soil bears fruit—but it bears *one hundred fold*. For those who have ears to hear, Jesus offered this incredible vision of possibility. When we bear fruit, it can nourish others for generations to come.

5. Review 8:16–18.

It seems like Jesus made a hard pivot when He went from talking about seeds and soil to lamps and jars, but He was driving home the same concept.

6. Read Matthew 5:16. In your own words, summarize Jesus's statement about light and good works.

Jesus often uses light and good works—or fruit—together. Just as fire and light take over everything they touch, and fruit contains seeds to grow more fruit, Jesus reiterated this multiplication principle: Those who seek God will accumulate more of who God is. And on the other hand, those who turn a deaf ear will experience a multiplied loss.

7. Fill in the gaps in Jesus's warning in 8:18:

"_____ _____ then how _____ _____."

8. What do you need to listen more carefully to in His Word today?

9. **Review 8:19–21.**

The crowd that surrounded Jesus prevented His mother and brothers from easily reaching Him. He used the opportunity to make a point—not to downplay biological family, but to upgrade all those in the family of God. Jesus elevated the eternal bond in a time when the nuclear family was often considered the most important part of a person's identity.

10. We often find our identity in our relationships. What secondary identities distract you from remembering your primary identity as a beloved child of God?

11. **Review 8:22–25.**

The disciples were among those Jesus had called to be in the eternal family of God, but they still had much to learn about this Savior-Man. He asked them to follow Him into a boat to go to the other side of the Sea of Galilee. The "other side" was the pagan side, and the sea between the two sides was known to erupt in storms without warning. Two dangerous scenarios—yet Jesus called His disciples directly into them.

12. What scary scenarios are you facing today? Write a short prayer asking God to calm your heart in that space.

Luke 8:26–56

READ LUKE 8:26–56

1. On the map below, circle Capernaum, Jesus's home base, and Gergesa (also known as Gerasenes).

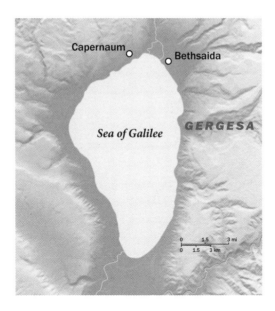

2. The western half of the Sea of Galilee was considered the Jewish side; the eastern half was considered the Gentile (non-Jewish) side. Which group of people lived in Gergesa/Gerasenes?

3. Review 8:26–39.

When Jesus and His disciples landed ashore on the Gentile side of the Sea of Galilee, they found a demonized man who was so overwhelmed by the demons that he was driven to live naked in a graveyard. Jesus and His disciples were going even deeper into the terrifying places they'd spent their whole lives avoiding. And they were facing a powerful enemy whose very name—Legion—suggested that the disciples were outnumbered. But as the Savior approached the demonized man, his tormentors were held to account.

4. What title did the demons give Jesus in 8:28?

Upon seeing Jesus, the man filled with demons fell on the ground and the demons acknowledged Him as the "Son of the Most High God." Though His disciples hadn't even grasped His true identity yet, the demons knew Him immediately, and they knew their place was to kneel before Him and beg for mercy. When He cast them out of the man, He agreed to send them into a herd of pigs, and the pigs immediately hurled themselves off the edge of a cliff and into the sea.

The formerly demon-possessed man sat at Jesus's feet, clothed and in his right mind. Meanwhile, the pig farmers must have experienced a variety of emotions—astonishment at the miracle, fear at Jesus's power, and anger over losing their source of income. Their fear took prominence, and they asked Jesus to leave.

The only person whose heart was changed and who longed for Jesus was the man to whom Jesus had extended grace. He asked to follow Jesus like the other disciples. Instead, Jesus gave him a new calling—He commissioned him to be His mouthpiece in the Gerasenes, and the man set out to tell others what Jesus had done for him.

5. When was the last time you shared the story of God's grace with someone new? How did that feel?

6. **Review 8:40–56.**

Upon returning to Capernaum, Jesus was approached by a ruler named Jairus whose daughter was sick. As Jesus was on His way to heal her, He was interrupted by a woman who had been bleeding for twelve years. She touched Him and she was healed! Jesus could have continued on His way, but He stopped to acknowledge the woman and praise her for her faith.

Though you may believe God is preoccupied with more important things than your circumstances, He is always attentive to your needs. And as the woman was experiencing that truth—possibly for the first time in her life—Jairus may have begun to question it. In the brief moments it took for Jesus to heal the bleeding woman, the man received word that his sick daughter had passed away.

The family had already admitted defeat and were mourning her death as Jesus approached the house, but Jesus—not bound by the natural world—brought her back to life. Before He left He charged the family to tell no one what had happened.

7. Why were His instructions to the demonized man (8:39) different from His response to the parents of the healed child (8:56)? **Use a commentary or study Bible for help.**

The Jewish-Gentile divide in first-century Israel can't be overstated. The fact that Jesus traveled into Gentile territory to reveal Himself as the Savior-God (the Gentiles weren't looking for a Messiah) demonstrated He was the Savior for all people. And for His message to continue spreading among the Gentiles while He lived primarily among the Jews, He commissioned Gentiles with the message.

Among the Jews, however, the Pharisees and Sadducees saw Him as a threat to their power and authority. Their mistaken expectations about a political and revolutionary savior could make Jesus's ministry much more difficult. So to continue on His mission to spread the news of the gospel, Jesus needed the message to travel at a lower volume. His timing and plan were carried out with precision.

Luke 9:1–17

READ LUKE 9:1–17

1. **Review 9:1–6, and fill in the chart below.**

	What Jesus Did	What Jesus Gave	What Jesus Empowered the Disciples to Do
9:1			
9:2			

You can't give what you don't have. If Jesus hadn't had power and authority, He couldn't have given it to them. God is still in the business of equipping those He calls. Whatever He initiates He will sustain and He will fulfill!

2. What five specific things did He tell them not to pack for their trip?

As He sent them out, He was teaching them to trust Him in both the spiritual and natural realms. What they were giving to the world they were also learning for themselves. If they didn't trust God, how could they tell others to trust Him?

3. In what areas of life do you have the hardest time trusting God to provide?

Jesus knew that some would hear the truth and not believe, so He gave instructions for when—not if—that happened: They should leave and not even take the dust with them! It's worth noting that God didn't promise obedience would lead to their desired outcome. Success was measured by their faithfulness to Jesus, not the responses of others.

4. Describe a time when you were obedient to God and it didn't lead to your desired outcome. How was your faith strengthened through that experience?

5. **Review 9:7–9.**

As they were fulfilling their calling throughout the region, word spread to Herod—the local governor who beheaded JTB. Imagine his confusion when some began to say that the leader of these apostles was the resurrected JTB! Other locals claimed Jesus was a resurrected prophet—perhaps even Elijah. Herod wanted to get to the bottom of the mystery, so he hoped to get face-to-face with Jesus.

6. Review 9:10–17.

The apostles returned to Capernaum, and Jesus took them by boat to the nearby village of Bethsaida, on the northern tip of the Sea of Galilee. Mark's gospel says He was taking them on a bit of a retreat to bless them after their hard work (Mark 6:30–33), but the crowds followed Jesus there.

7. What do you think: Was Jesus planning a retreat that was disrupted by the crowd? Or was it part of Jesus's plan to minister to the people while they were there?

Without a pause, He continued to preach the kingdom and heal the sick—working again in both the spiritual and natural realms. Toward the end of the day, the disciples wanted to send the crowds away, but Jesus saw a possibility they didn't have eyes to see. He leaned into the need and invited the apostles into the process, multiplying five loaves and two fish to feed an estimated fifteen thousand people (five thousand men, plus women and children)!

8. When was the last time God did something that exceeded your capabilities—perhaps something that didn't even occur to you to pray for because it seemed so impossible?

After feeding the crowds, the apostles collected twelve baskets of leftovers—one for each apostle. Though they'd been hesitant to participate, their yes to Jesus resulted in a multiplied blessing for everyone involved. Their service was not only a blessing to others but a blessing to them as well!

9. **Using a Bible dictionary or commentary, look up the symbolism of the number twelve and write down what you find.**

Within Jewish communities, including where this miracle occurred, the number twelve held great significance. It represented completion, and it was the number of Israel's tribes. In the early days of His ministry, Jesus and His apostles—who were likely from only a handful of the twelve tribes—sent this miraculous, symbolic message that His provision was for *all* the tribes of Israel. Jesus used the few to bless the many. He used the little to bless the whole. Though you may feel like your calling is small or insignificant, when your yes meets God's yes, there is no limit to what God can do through you and for you!

Luke 9:18–36

 **READ LUKE 9:18–36**

1. **Review 9:18–20.**

In today's reading, Jesus set the disciples up for an important revelation in one of His favorite ways: by asking a question. He asked them who the crowds thought He was. The general consensus was either JTB or Elijah—respected men who stood up to the rulers of their day. Those answers signal that perhaps the crowd was expecting Jesus to be a political messiah who would end the oppression from Rome. Jesus didn't ask this question because He was ignorant or didn't know the answer; He used it to set up a more important follow-up question: Who did the disciples think He was? Peter—ever eager to be in the heart of the action—answered for the group.

2. How did Peter describe Jesus in 9:20? How did Jesus respond?

They understood He was more than just a prophet—He was Israel's re-deemer, the promised Messiah.

3. **Review 9:21–22.**

After establishing His identity among His disciples, Jesus let them in on His plans. This is the first time in Luke's gospel that Jesus foretold His death. This would've dealt a heavy blow to their hopes and expectations for the Messiah—not only would He not be overthrowing the government authorities, but He would be rejected by the elders and chief priests and eventually killed. However, the story had another twist—one they wouldn't grasp for a long time but that would lead to their inextinguishable hope: He would be raised from the dead on the third day!

4. **Read 1 Peter 1:20 and Revelation 13:8.** How do these verses give you confidence in the life and death of Jesus?

Jesus's death was not an accident or a backup plan—it has been *the* plan since before the invention of time itself. While this appeared to be bad news for the apostles, it was the means by which God was working out His orderly plan.

5. **Review 9:23–27.** Oftentimes when Jesus referred to His coming sacrificial death, He followed those statements with a teaching for the disciples.

What do you think: Why would Jesus give a teaching on this topic after referencing His death and resurrection?

Jesus took the disciples on a roller coaster of emotions. First, He revealed that He would die, but then He revealed that He would rise again. Did that mean life in the kingdom of the resurrected Jesus would be lush and easy? No. Even though His kingdom would not end with His death, the lives of those in His kingdom wouldn't be easy.

6. Match Jesus's instructions for His followers with the corresponding meaning:

"Deny himself"	Be willing to face rejection and possibly death.
"Take up his cross"	Preach the gospel; abide by His teachings
"Follow me"	Give up personal control of your own life

These are all incredibly challenging callings associated with loss and pain—but in the scope of eternity, even His "taking" is giving (9:24).

7. Using your favorite Bible commentary, research the meaning of Jesus's words in 9:27.

8. **Review 9:28–36.**

About a week later, Jesus took three disciples up to a mountain where they witnessed the clear answer to the previous question. These select disciples—Peter, James, and John—had the unique privilege of seeing Jesus's transfiguration. His face and clothes changed as Moses and Elijah appeared, representing the Old Testament law and the prophets. Their presence alongside Jesus proved two things. First, the theory that He could be Elijah couldn't possibly be true since they were present simultaneously. Second, Jesus is the fulfillment of the law and prophecies the Old Testament outlined. As if that weren't proof enough, the voice of God the Father erupted from a cloud, affirming the identity of Jesus as His beloved Son.

9. What was the Father's command after He identified Jesus? Why do you think He included these words?

Elijah and Moses were great men who had key roles in the Old Testament, but Jesus is the culmination of the plan set before the beginning of time. He is the one they spoke about. And He is the one we should bend our lives to follow.

Luke 9:37–62

✝ READ LUKE 9:37-62

Not long after Peter, James, and John witnessed Jesus's transfiguration, the disciples encountered several scenarios where they seemed to misunderstand the role they played in the kingdom. As Jesus revealed more about His identity, the disciples may have felt a sense of superiority and it seems they even ranked themselves.

1. **Review 9:37–43a.**

In this passage, we met a father who was desperate to help his demonized son. Some of the disciples had already tried and failed to cast out this demon.

2. Why did they fail? **Look up Matthew's account of this story (Matthew 17:14–20) for help.**

Despite their zeal, the disciples weren't always successful at performing miracles. Sometimes their inability corresponded to a lack of faith, prayer, or fasting. Those spiritual disciplines don't make us *worthier* to perform miracles; however, they serve as reminders that we don't operate in our own power. Any strength we may demonstrate is a result of His presence in us. Jesus, on the other hand, immediately cast out the demon.

3. Review 9:43b–45.

Before the crowd could pick their chins up off the floor, Jesus took the disciples for another loop on the roller coaster ride. In the midst of this beautiful miracle, He brought up His death a second time. He spoke the truth plainly, again, but the disciples still didn't fully understand—in fact, Scripture says His meaning was "concealed" (*parakalyptō*) from them. This is the only time this Greek word appears in Scripture.

4. What do you think: How and why would this be "concealed from them"? Why might that have been an important part of their experience as disciples?

5. Review 9:46–48.

Having missed the point, it's no surprise they got caught up in an argument over which one of them was the greatest. Because Jesus was the Messiah, it's likely they felt entitled to positions of status in His kingdom. But He corrected them using an unexpected illustration to reorient their perspective.

6. How were little children viewed and/or treated in ancient Israel?

While elders were esteemed in the ancient Near East, children were disregarded, had no social status, and were unaware of riches or power. The disciples fought to be praised and gain recognition, but Jesus challenged them to pursue humility and a spirit of hospitality.

7. Take an honest look at the spaces and people you regularly encounter. Where in your life might you be angling for recognition or position? How can you turn that into an opportunity to be more others-focused?

8. **Review 9:49–50.**

On the heels of the disciples' lack of success with casting out the demons, it's possible John was carrying some frustration. And because insecurity often manifests as arrogance, this may have led John to stop a man who was casting out demons in Jesus's name. But Jesus pointed out that there was no need for a mindset of division or competition, because the man was on their team!

9. **Review 9:51–56.**

Luke flashes forward to give us another example of a time when the disciples overstepped their position. This event took place later in Jesus's ministry, but it fits with Luke's theme here. When a Samaritan village refused to welcome Jesus, James and John offered to call down fire from heaven as a punishment on them, but Jesus denied them and continued on His way.

10. **Review 9:57–62.**

In today's final scene, Luke wraps up by pointing out that, contrary to the view that the life of a disciple was filled with glory and honor, following Jesus wasn't glamorous. Jesus encountered three people who said they'd follow Him, but they all had a caveat—something they wanted to take care of first.

11. Summarize Jesus's responses to the three people who wanted to follow Him.

1.

2.

3.

At first glance, Jesus's responses may seem harsh or cruel. However, He was acknowledging that following Him means we may have to miss out on things we think of as good. Consider yesterday's message about denying ourselves, taking up our cross, and following Him.

Discipleship is not a power grab, and it's not an easy path. Alongside the great revelations—like witnessing the transfiguration—it's important to remember that the life of the disciple is about esteeming Him above everything else. As theologian Matthew Henry wrote, quoting his father, "He is no fool who parts with that which he cannot keep, when he is sure to be recompensed with that which he cannot lose."* Jesus is the ultimate treasure—He's where the joy is!

12. What stood out to you most in this week's study? Why?

13. What did you learn or relearn about God and His character this week?

* Philip Henry, quoted in Matthew Henry, *The Complete Works of the Rev. Matthew Henry; (His Unfinished Commentary Excepted): Being a Collection of All His Treatises, Sermons, and Tracts, as Published by Himself: and a Memoir of His Life*, vol. 2 (London: A. Fullarton and Co., 1853), 634.

Corresponding Psalm & Prayer

 **READ PSALM 127**

1. What correlation do you see between Psalm 127 and this week's study of Jesus as Savior?

2. What portions of this psalm stand out to you most?

3. Close by praying this prayer aloud:

Father,
   You sent Your Son to fulfill the law and prophets, and You affirmed His divinity with Your own voice. You sent Him to save, and yet,

You sent Him to serve—to heal the sick and feed the crowds. You are more awesome, more wonderful, more complex than my finite mind could ever comprehend, and I praise You with my whole heart!

I confess that I've lost sight of who You are and who I am. I have argued—if not aloud, then in my head—with my brothers and sisters about who is the greatest in Your kingdom. I have insisted that my works have earned me a seat at Your table. I have forgotten that without Your blessing, every second of my striving has been for myself. Forgive me.

Teach me, like You taught Solomon, that unless You are in it, it's in vain. Show me, like Jesus showed His apostles, that unless You provide it, it's worthless. Help my work to come not from a spirit of anxious greed, but from a heart of faithful obedience. May the result of my limited work be limitless because of You. May the work You do through me bear fruit one hundredfold! If I boast in anything, let it be You!

I surrender my life to You, Lord—every moment of my day, each decision I make, I yield my will and way to Your perfect will and way.

I love You too. Amen.

Rest, Catch Up, or Dig Deeper

⚔ WEEKLY CHALLENGE

On Day 2, we asked, "When was the last time you shared the story of God's grace with someone new? How did that feel?" This week, open up a conversation about your faith with someone new. You don't necessarily have to ask them about their faith, although you certainly can. This practice is just to help you learn the practice of sharing the story of God's grace with someone else. Aim to make this less of a story about the before-and-after of how *you* have changed, and more of a story about Jesus and His grace toward you and His finished work on the cross. What did it look like for your heart to be captured by the story of His love?

Luke 10–11:

The Focus of the Savior

DAILY BIBLE READING

Day 1. Luke 10:1–24

Day 2. Luke 10:25–42

Day 3. Luke 11:1–13

Day 4. Luke 11:14–32

Day 5. Luke 11:33–54

Day 6. Psalm 3

Day 7. Catch-Up Day

Corresponds to Days 298 and 286 of *The Bible Recap.*

WEEKLY CHALLENGE

See page 153 for more information.

Luke 10:1–24

READ LUKE 10:1-24

1. **Review 10:1–12.**

Earlier, Jesus sent out the twelve apostles; in today's reading, He commissioned an additional seventy-two of His followers for ministry. They were appointed to go ahead of time to the places Jesus planned to visit. To prepare them, He gave them instructions that shared a lot of overlap with what He'd told the first dozen men (9:1–6)—travel light in dependence on God's provision, preach the good news, bring healing, and testify against those who reject the message. But Jesus gave some added perspective and expanded directions to this second group of ambassadors.

2. What harvest was Jesus referring to in 10:2? What was the state of the harvest and the adjacent issue? What was His proposed solution?

Jesus shared some great news with a caveat: There was no lack of souls ready to be reaped for eternal life; however, there was a shortage of people willing to participate in the work. He was sending out six times as many people as before, but the need was still great. The words translated in the ESV as "pray earnestly" come from the Greek word *deomai*.

3. **Using a Greek lexicon or a concordance, write the meaning of *deomai* below.** Find the five other verses where it has shown up so far in Luke's gospel.

4. When have you *deomai*-ed God for something? Have those prayers been more eternally or temporally focused?

Jesus charged the seventy-two to plead with God to multiply the workforce even as they obediently joined the efforts. He was telling them how to be part of the answer to their own prayer! Then, He made the serious and urgent nature of the work clear. They were going out like prey in predator territory, carrying a message about the nearness of the kingdom. This specific mission was so weighty that they were told to avoid pleasantries along the way. Blessing was in store for the people who received them, while judgment was being stored up for the towns that rejected them.

5. **Review 10:13–16.**

Jesus specifically called out Chorazin, Bethsaida, and Capernaum—these were cities in the Galilee region that had witnessed many of His powerful acts, yet hadn't turned in repentance to receive salvation. In contrast, Tyre and Sidon were sinful cities condemned in the Old Testament, yet Jesus said they would've responded rightly if they'd seen the same things. A modern parallel might be something like this: "I did miracles from the pulpit on Sunday morning, but the churchgoers didn't repent. If I'd done those same miracles in the club on Saturday night, the whole place would've turned from their wicked ways and followed Me!"

6. **Review 10:16 and read Romans 10:11–17.** What can you take away from these passages about the importance of Jesus's representatives sharing His message?

7. **Review 10:17–20.** When the seventy-two returned, what did they express joy over? How did Jesus address it?

8. What does it mean that their names "are written in heaven," and why would Jesus direct them toward this as a better source of joy?

In 10:18, Jesus made a statement some scholars interpret differently. By referencing Satan falling like lightning, some think Jesus was talking about the initial rebellious fall of the former angel (which had already happened), while others believe He was foretelling Satan's final defeat. Either way, Jesus acknowledged that the authority He had given—which the seventy-two had exercised—was incredible. Satan and his team of spiritual forces were no match for God's power, and those who were sent out witnessed that firsthand!

However, what was to bring them the most joy wasn't those spiritual abilities or experiences—it was their status as those who had received Him as Savior. Their names were recorded on God's heavenly roster of eternal life! Above any achievement or identity we can claim—spiritual or otherwise—having a relationship with Jesus as the Savior of our souls should bring us the greatest joy.

9. What titles, achievements, or relationships are you tempted to celebrate as much as (or even elevated over) your relationship with Jesus?

10. **Review 10:21–24.**

The Father's will is to reveal Jesus as Savior to people who come to Him like children with humble hearts to receive, and to conceal the truth from those who, in their pride, believe they already have all the answers. Jesus rejoiced in this as a gracious act and blessing from the Father.

11. What had the disciples seen and heard that prophets and kings of Israel's past longed to experience?

If you're a Christ-follower, you share in this same blessing. You know the Savior because of the gracious will of God and through the work of laborers He has sent into His fields across the ages!

Luke 10:25–42

READ LUKE 10:25-42

1. **Review 10:25–37.** Fill in the chart below.

Verse	Summarize the question in your own words.	What's the motive for asking?	What might the question and/or motive point to about his heart?
10:25			
10:29			

2. Look up information about the role and status of a first-century Jewish lawyer. How does what you found help frame this man's interaction with Jesus?

The lawyer in this text wasn't an attorney specializing in prosecution, defense, or complicated contracts like we might think of today. This lawyer knew the Torah—God's holy law given to the Jews—inside and out. He was a likely candidate for the ranks of the "wise and understanding" whom Jesus referenced in 10:21. His agenda was to challenge Jesus and validate himself as righteous before God, but Jesus took things in a different direction.

Jesus turned the first question around, giving the man an opportunity to answer from his knowledge of the Scriptures. The man quoted Deuteronomy 6:5 and Leviticus 19:18, and Jesus approved; loving God with one's entire being and loving others as yourself summarized the entirety of God's law. Anyone who could do those two things would be given the blessing of eternal life.

3. Consider your thoughts, attitudes, actions, and interactions over the past week. For every day you perfectly fulfilled Luke 10:27 draw a check mark. Draw an X for every day you failed.

☐ Sunday

☐ Monday

☐ Tuesday

☐ Wednesday

☐ Thursday

☐ Friday

☐ Saturday

If you checked all seven boxes *and* could check all boxes representing every other day of your life—past and future—Jesus says you've qualified yourself for eternal life! Easy enough, right? (Obviously not.)

Instead of acknowledging that the bar set for inheriting eternal life was higher than he could reach, the lawyer moved on to the technicalities of keeping the law. Jesus redirected the conversation and confronted the lawyer's underlying heart issues through a parable.

4. Fill in the chart below regarding the people who encountered the half-dead man in the ditch.

Verse(s)	Description of person	Summarize their response
10:31		
10:32		
10:33–35		

5. **In a commentary or study Bible, read about each of the three.** Using only the terms *righteous* or *unrighteous*, label each according to how the lawyer and Jews would have perceived them based on background and affiliations. Then, label them according to what their actions reflect.

Character #1 Title / Identifier (10:31): _____

Public perception: _____

Actions: _____

Character #2 Title / Identifier (10:32): _____

Public perception: _____

Actions: _____

Character #3 Title / Identifier (10:33): _____

Public perception: _____

Actions: _____

The self-assured lawyer was looking for a legal out that would exempt him from having to love certain people. He came asking "Who is my neighbor?" and left with a lesson on how to be a neighbor. Jesus showed that true, God-honoring, law-fulfilling, neighborly love was marked by extravagant compassion and sacrificial service and included even those considered enemies.

The lawyer acknowledged that the merciful Samaritan in the parable was the one who demonstrated God's heart behind the law, and Jesus told the lawyer to live the same way.

Often, our instinct is to think about how we should be more like the good Samaritan, and that's a good thing to consider. But the better thing to consider is how Jesus the Savior has been the good Samaritan to us—the man in the ditch who cannot help himself.

6. List the parallels you see between the good Samaritan's actions and the realities of your salvation through Christ. Attach corresponding Scripture where you can.

Samaritan's Actions	Christ's Saving of Me	Scripture

The high bar set for inheriting salvation is one Jesus alone can clear on our behalf. Growing in the ability to love God and show mercy to others starts when we acknowledge our failure and our inability to keep God's commands. As we embrace that reality, we move into repentance and receive His love and mercy through faith.

7. **Review 10:38–42.** Why do you think Martha might have expected Jesus to correct Mary?

It made sense for Martha to launch into serving mode. She was hosting an honored guest in her home and was faithfully fulfilling a cultural expectation. Mary, on the other hand, was doing something many would consider scandalous.

In writing that Mary "sat at the Lord's feet" (10:39), Luke wasn't just describing her physical position; he was using a phrase that indicated *she was postured as a learning disciple*. The same language is used in Acts 22:3 when the apostle Paul said that he was "educated at the feet of Gamaliel." It was unheard of for a woman to be taught the things of God in that day. Jesus, however, was in the business of defying norms and establishing the culture of the kingdom. He embraced and affirmed Mary's action! And in His kindness, He saw Martha working hard to serve—an important responsibility that had likely been ingrained in her as the best thing she could be doing—and invited her to join her sister in *something better*.

Luke's is the only gospel that includes this narrative, and it's yet another instance of Luke's commitment to emphasize that women aren't marginal to God or an afterthought to Him—they are included and valued!

8. What things in your life, including good and important ones, tend to distract you from "the good portion" of learning from God's Word and time in His presence? How does it impact you to remember that Jesus said that portion is the one necessary thing and cannot be taken away?

Luke 11:1–13

✝ READ LUKE 11:1-13

Prayer was a regular part of Jewish religious practice, but Jesus's disciples noticed something distinct about His prayers that led them to conclude they still had much to learn. They asked Him to teach them what He knew.

The phrase "more is caught than taught" describes the reality that a lot can be gained from attentive observation. Instruction is helpful, but the lived experience often has a deeper impact.

1. As you've read the Bible and spent time learning from the life of Jesus, what have you "caught" from His example and how has it affected your perspective or practice of prayer?

2. Who in your life has modeled prayer in a way that you've been encouraged or challenged by? What did you learn from them? Be specific. Then thank God for them!

In response to their request, Jesus shared what's now called the Lord's Prayer with His disciples. (Matthew's gospel records a lengthier version of this prayer in Matthew 6:9–13.)

Jesus laid the foundation for prayer by speaking to God the Father. The fact that we are directed to speak to God the Father is an incredible blessing! Jesus was leading the disciples to remember their position as God's beloved children. *Father* carried the connotation of intimacy and love toward them *as well as* His authority over them.

3. Why is it important for believers to hold both of those realities when we pray?

While there are many great ways we could analyze the rest of Jesus's modeled prayer, let's focus on two specific elements: declarations and requests.

4. **Using a commentary, study Bible, or other resources, fill in the charts below.**

Declarations made about God	Meaning/Summary	Significance/ Personal Implication
"Hallowed be your name"		
"Your kingdom come"		

Requests Made of God	Meaning/Summary	Significance/ Personal Implication
11:3 _____		
11:4 _____		
11:4 _____		

The declarations centered around honoring God and acknowledging His reign and the priority of the kingdom—inaugurated through Jesus's ministry (Luke 10:9) and headed toward its final form (Revelation 11:15–17). The requests pointed to Him as a provider who meets physical and spiritual needs, as well as a protector and guide in the face of the temptations of this world. Jesus didn't just make up something that sounded good—He knew exactly how His followers needed to be oriented in their thoughts about God, and He taught them accordingly.

It's easy and natural for us to pray in ways that are very different from His example. Believers should come to God with love and reverence, in daily dependence, and as champions of His kingdom agenda. But we often show up inconsistently, robotically, and irreverently, toting self-centered wish lists.

5. Using Jesus's model as an outline, write your own short prayer that could serve as a model for yourself and/or others.

As Jesus continued His teaching on prayer, He gave an illustration of a host with a big dilemma by Middle Eastern hospitality standards: a hungry out-of-town visitor and an empty pantry.

6. Why did the "friend" respond to the request of the desperate host? **(Hint: Look up the word *impudence*.)**

Jesus encouraged His disciples to pray with persistence: asking, seeking, and knocking, which leads to receiving, finding, and opened doors. An annoyed man would get out of bed to meet the needs of a relentless neighbor, and a flawed earthly father would grant his kid's requests for good things that were within his means. Doesn't it stand to reason that God, as a perfect heavenly Father, would far exceed those standards by both responding to prayer *and* blessing His children?

In wisdom and love, God doesn't give us everything we ask for, because He alone knows what is good for us both now and eternally. Just like the father in 11:11–12 *would* give good things like a fish or an egg to a child who asked, God *won't* give us the "serpents" and "scorpions" we ask for just because we ask Him. But we can trust that He hears us and is committed to giving us incredible gifts, such as the Holy Spirit!

7. **Read John 14:15–17; 14:25–26; Romans 8:12–17; and Ephesians 1:3–14.** Why is the Holy Spirit one of the best gifts God could give you?

Luke 11:14–32

 **READ LUKE 11:14-32**

1. **Review 11:14–23.**

Various mighty works accompanied the words Jesus spoke about salvation. They served as visual aids for the invisible spiritual realities He'd come to reveal. The mute man He'd delivered from a demon was a walking, talking miracle, and he served as evidence to back up the message that Jesus was the Savior God sent to the world.

2. What testimonies or transformation stories have you heard, seen, or experienced that point others to Jesus? Does a specific instance come to mind? Briefly describe it.

People were dumbfounded by what Jesus had done, yet their responses didn't add up. Some who witnessed the exorcism said Jesus was operating under the demonic power of Satan. Others weren't willing to give their final verdict and demanded that Jesus do something more to prove Himself. Matthew 12:24 identifies the naysayers in this account as Pharisees. Jesus had encountered their unbelief repeatedly yet was still willing to respond to their accusations.

3. Summarize the points and illustration Jesus used as His defense.

Point #1 (11:17–18):

Point #2 (11:19):

Illustration (11:21–22):

In a section that could be called "A Tale of Two Kingdoms," Jesus confronted His opposers' absurdity and bias. First, Satan's self-sabotage made no sense. Second, if the miracle had been performed by the hands of someone else—one of their own followers or "sons," for instance—they would've accepted the work as divine without hesitation.

Satan—whom Scripture calls the god and ruler of this world (2 Corinthians 4:4, John 12:31)—is strong, but Jesus, the king of heaven and earth, is stronger. Jesus drew a line in the sand between the two kingdoms: Either you were part of His kingdom, working to gather people to God through salvation, or you were part of Satan's opposing kingdom, scattering people away from true life.

4. **Review 11:24–28.** What was Jesus's warning about? What significance might the additional number of demons have?

All the talk of demonic activity in this text could understandably raise questions or fear. While Scripture teaches that Satan and demonic activity are real, it also teaches that the enemy is on a leash. God is sovereign over even His enemies. It's important to hold both realities simultaneously—to be neither overly fixated on the demonic nor dismissive of its power.

5. Do you tend to swing to one extreme or the other when it comes to a view of the demonic? If so, which one?

Our greatest source of spiritual protection also happens to be the way we can access great blessings. By listening to and obeying God's commandments and instructions, we can be kept safe from Satan's schemes (Ephesians 6:10–18) and receive a blessing even better than being chosen to bear the Savior of the world (Luke 11:27–28)! Wow!

6. **Review 11:29–32.**

Jesus referenced two Old Testament accounts to explain why the people's rejection of Him was a big deal.

7. **Look up the accounts Jesus mentioned, read the passages, and fill in the chart below.**

	Similarities with Jesus	Differences from Jesus
Solomon and the Queen of the South/Sheba (1 Kings 10:1–10)		
Jonah and the people of Nineveh (Jonah 3:1–10)		

8. **Look up the word *condemn*.** If Jesus is the one who will judge the world for sin, in what sense would the queen of the South or the men of Nineveh be able to condemn that generation?

It isn't bad to think of new ways to help people encounter the truth, but we can wrongly believe that having more compelling evidence or more relevant and eloquent presentations will lead to more belief. Jesus made it clear that His ministry and teaching were more than enough to convict of sin and lead to repentance.

9. **Read Romans 1:15–17 and 2 Corinthians 2:15.** How can these truths shape your perspective on sharing the gospel with others?

The gospel message found on the pages of Scripture is powerful enough to convict of sin, reveal Jesus, and lead even the hardest of hearts to repentance and faith! For many of us, it's easy to think of this in broad terms, but we may be less convinced of the possibility of salvation for the worst people we can imagine. Do you struggle to believe that simply encountering the gospel could transform anyone specific? The message the Savior of the world came to deliver is that His death and resurrection are sufficient for all those who come to Him!

Luke 11:33–54

 **READ LUKE 11:33-54**

1. **Review 11:33–36.** How do Jesus's words here connect back to 11:29–32?

Jesus was sent into the world to illuminate the way out of darkness, and His mission was far from top secret. He preached in front of crowds, taught in synagogues, publicly revealed divine power, and openly identified as Savior. When people, like the Pharisees, failed to recognize His light and respond accordingly, the issue was never that Jesus was a dim or obscured lamp, but that their vision was faulty.

2. Jesus gave the warning to "be careful lest the light in you be darkness" (11:35). How can you discern whether your spiritual eyes are in good or bad health? Be specific.

When Jesus was invited to share a meal with a Pharisee and his friends, He used it as an opportunity to shed more light on the issue of being in spiritual darkness.

3. **Review 11:37–41.** What did Jesus do that shocked His host? Why was it a big deal?

Jesus was knowingly defying one of the Pharisees' elaborate purification customs. The practice wasn't something God commanded, but they believed those who didn't observe it were defiled. They expected Jesus to adhere to their tradition. This was one example of thousands of traditions in the oral law.

The Pharisees were obsessed with external appearances while being inattentive to the state of their hearts. They had misdirected zeal and a false sense of righteousness, and Jesus wanted them to know those things didn't translate to a righteous standing before God. If they had addressed their real issue, they could've experienced the authentic transformation of their whole being.

4. In His ministry, Jesus showed patience, gentleness, and compassion to a wide array of people in the midst of their sin and lack of understanding. However, He often dealt with the Pharisees, lawyers, and scribes more harshly. Why do you think this was the case?

5. Review 11:42–52.

Jesus highlighted specific symptoms of heart disease in the Pharisees and lawyers. Both were headed for a sad fate if they didn't change course.

6. Match each of the six woes Jesus pronounced with what the Pharisees or lawyers were guilty of. Use the provided cross-references if needed.

Woes to Pharisees

_____ 11:42 (Micah 6:8)

_____ 11:43 (Matthew 23:5–7)

_____ 11:44 (Numbers 19:14–16)

Woes to Lawyers

_____ 11:46 (Acts 15:10–11)

_____ 11:47–51 (Acts 7:51–52)

_____ 11:52 (Malachi 2:7–8)

Their Sin

A. Hypocrisy

B. Rejecting God's revelation

C. Lack of compassion and mercy

D. Pride and self-promotion

E. Legalism

F. Keeping people from true understanding

G. Failing to obey God's command

H. Leading people toward impurity instead of righteousness

The leaders had dishonored God and negatively impacted His people. They were hidden sources of spiritual contamination and obstructed the true meaning of God's law when they had the responsibility to make things clear. They may have celebrated God's messengers from the past, but they were just as guilty as the wicked men who had murdered those messengers, because they were persecuting Jesus, who was the very culmination of each of those prophets' ministries! Despite all their underhanded, wicked ways, they maintained spiritual esteem from those around them.

Like those Jesus confronted, Christians can have an appearance of godliness that is vastly different from what God sees.

7. Pause. Ask God to reveal any inconsistencies between the reputation you try to maintain and your actual character (your motives, thoughts, what you do behind closed doors, etc.). Are there areas where you aren't walking in integrity? Get honest with yourself.

8. If so, write out a prayer asking the Holy Spirit to help you live as someone who doesn't just look clean but is washed clean.

9. **Review 11:53–54.** How did the religious leaders respond to Jesus's rebuke? What would've been a better response?

Being exposed to the light of Christ after living in darkness can be jarring and even painful. One option is to keep our eyes shut to avoid the discomfort of conviction. The other option is to behold and esteem the Savior of our souls, allowing His Spirit to redirect us. We can walk in confidence that anything He has for us is better than anything we could leave behind—because He's where the joy is!

10. What stood out to you most in this week's study? Why?

11. What did you learn or relearn about God and His character this week?

Corresponding Psalm & Prayer

 **READ PSALM 3**

1. What correlation do you see between Psalm 3 and this week's study of Jesus as Savior?

2. What portions of this psalm stand out to you most?

3. Close by praying this prayer aloud:

Father,

   Your name is hallowed and holy. You are the giver and sustainer of life. You give salvation. You are my glory and the one who lifts my head when I despair!

I repent because I haven't loved You with all my heart, soul, and strength, and I haven't loved my neighbor as myself. I've used cultural norms or my own interpretation of Your law to justify ignoring the man bleeding in the ditch. I've used well-intended service as an excuse to forgo something better: time with You.

As I lie down, sleep, and wake, may I—like David—know that You are the one sustaining me. And like Your Son instructed the seventy-two to do, prompt me to join in the work of Your harvest. And please, Father, send colaborers!

As we, the colaborers, work together for You, remind us that salvation belongs to You. When we're discouraged, remind us that You alone can change hearts. When we're doubtful, remind us that You can change even the hardest of those hearts. As Your Son taught us to pray, "Your kingdom come."

I surrender my life to You, Lord—every moment of my day, each decision I make, I yield my will and way to Your perfect will and way.

I love You too. Amen.

Rest, Catch Up, or Dig Deeper

✝ WEEKLY CHALLENGE

On Day 1, we saw Jesus encourage His followers to "pray earnestly" (10:2) regarding the salvation of the lost. The Greek word He used (*deomai*) loosely translates to "beg." Make a list of at least five people you know who would not identify as Christians. Set a timer for each day this week at a time when you can spend five minutes *deomai*-ing God for their salvation. If you have five people on your list, that amounts to one minute per person each day. Pray specifically for them, by name, asking God to bless them, soften their heart, give them a holy curiosity about Him, surround them with joyful people who know and love Jesus, and grant them repentance. This week we practice *begging God* to save these souls!

Luke 12–14:
The Position of the Savior

DAILY BIBLE READING

Day 1. Luke 12:1–34

Day 2. Luke 12:35–59

Day 3. Luke 13:1–21

Day 4. Luke 13:22–35

Day 5. Luke 14

Day 6. Psalm 147

Day 7. Catch-Up Day

Corresponds to Days 299–300 of *The Bible Recap.*

WEEKLY CHALLENGE

See page 180 for more information.

Luke 12:1–34

✝ READ LUKE 12:1-34

Even though many people were following Jesus by this point in His ministry, today's reading gave us a series of sidebars where He issued warnings to His disciples that He didn't always give to the broader crowd.

1. Review 12:1–3.

His first warning was about the Pharisees, whose hypocrisy spread through everything they did. He compared it to leaven, a fermented dough used to help bread rise—it only takes a small amount to affect the whole loaf. If leaven is mixed into a loaf, it will eventually be obvious to anyone who sees it—and the same goes for the heart motives of the Pharisees. Those would eventually be revealed as well.

Everything would come to light, in fact. Including the secrets that Jesus and His disciples had to speak at a low volume—things such as the messianic secret. Eventually they would be speaking those messages at full volume in public settings—from rooftops, even! (See also: Matthew 10:26–27.)

2. **Review 12:4–7.**

Then He encouraged (and warned) the disciples not to walk in fear of man. He had already talked about His coming persecution and death, but He knew most of them would also die as martyrs for their faith. But because God is attentive to even the smallest details—like birds and the hairs on our heads—He can certainly be trusted to provide for a person made in His image! They had no reason to fear those who could—and would—kill them.

3. According to 12:5, who should they fear instead of man? In your own words, how would you describe that fear—what does it look like on a practical level?

4. **Review 12:8–12.**

Though these words were spoken to the disciples, these principles (and for some, the realities) still apply to us today. Regardless of what we face as a result of our relationship with Jesus, God is with us. If we are put on trial for our faith, like the disciples were, He promises to be our confidence. In the face of persecution, He will equip us with what to say and do.

Just as much as there was a reward for the faithful, there was also a consequence for the faithless. Those who reject the Holy Spirit won't be forgiven. And as for those who deny Jesus—He will deny them in front of the angels. It's easy to acknowledge Jesus as Lord in our hearts or in our heads, but it's altogether different for our faith to be seen and heard.

5. If someone were to randomly poll a handful of people in your life and ask them about your relationship with Jesus, what would they say?

6. **Review 12:13–21.**

As Jesus was teaching, He encountered a man trying to get his brother to divide their father's inheritance with him. Jesus responded with a parable, one of His favorite forms of teaching. As a reminder, parables often have nameless characters, generalized details, and only one main point. This parable recounted a rich man stockpiling goods in his barns. When he didn't have enough room for his possessions, he tore down the barns to build bigger ones. He expected he'd be able to sit back and enjoy it all, but death came for him first. Jesus's message was clear: Our souls won't find true rest in possessions. This, too, served as a warning.

7. Regardless of the size of your bank account, do you ever find yourself thinking like the rich man? What's the last thing you bought thinking, *This will solve my problem!*, but that actually failed to satisfy you? How does this passage challenge you?

8. **Review 12:22–34.**

Per usual, Jesus spoke a more potent, direct message to the disciples specifically than to the crowd at large. He doubled down on His warnings against worrying and being anxious. For those who aren't Christ-followers, fear and anxiety are natural and fitting because they don't have God as their Father. But for those of us who are God's children (those who know Jesus as Savior), He promises that He's attentive to our every need.

9. Fill in the blanks from 12:32.

Fear not, little flock, for it is your Father's _____ _____ to give you ___ _____.

God has been so generous to us that we can extend that generosity to others! In fact, He encouraged His disciples to be willing to get rid of all their possessions. And while that message may have been specific to the disciples in their unique calling, the heart of the message remains the same to all believers: God will provide for you, so you can share. Because our heart bends toward whatever we invest in, we'd be wise to invest in the things—specifically the kingdom-related things—that we want to see take up *more* space in our hearts and lives and thoughts.

10. Is there a specific step of obedience you feel God calling you to take in response to today's study? If so, write it here:

Luke 12:35–59

✝ **READ LUKE 12:35-59**

In today's reading Jesus offered more warnings for the disciples. He shared a parable about living in eager anticipation of His return, but the theme was likely lost on the disciples. After all, He'd been talking about His death and they hadn't even grasped that reality yet, so they were still a long way off from understanding His resurrection, ascension, and second coming.

However, He set them up to understand it retrospectively, at a time when they'd need that information most. And since today we live in the "already but not yet" (after the resurrection but before His return), it serves us well too! He painted the picture of house servants who were awake and ready for their master to return from a wedding feast. The faithful servants who anticipated his return and prepared for it would be blessed.

1. **Review 12:35–40.** What hours are the second and third watches? Use a study Bible or do a web search for help.

In the time before doorbell cameras, watchmen operated in four separate three-hour shifts throughout the night to make sure a wealthy household stayed safe. However, these servants weren't merely staying awake; they were eagerly awaiting their master's return. In 12:40, He refers to the "Son of Man," one of His favorite names for Himself. He's boiling it down for them: *This parable is about Me and My return.*

2. Be honest with yourself: How often do you think of and eagerly anticipate the return of Jesus?

3. **Review 12:41–48.**

After Jesus referenced the Son of Man, Peter likely realized the parable was about Jesus. He interrupted and asked for greater clarity: "You're telling us this privately—just us disciples—so is this message just for us? Or is it for everyone?"

Jesus didn't answer directly, but as He continued the parable the answer became clearer: The disciples had been entrusted with a lot. As a result, much would be required of them. He was preparing them for the role they'd play after His ascension. They'd be the ones to lead the initial charge of planting churches and going out as missionaries. They would be blessed and granted even more!

The faithful and wise manager in this parable fulfilled his responsibilities, while the unfaithful servant believed his master was delayed in coming.

4. List the three ways the unfaithful servant spent his time when he assumed his master was delayed.

1.

2.

3.

As he forgot the long-term plan, he grew more angry and impatient, more selfish and debauched. For this unfaithful servant, there were severe consequences. And there were varying levels of unfaithfulness among other servants, and each was held to the standard of his knowledge and response.

5. **Review 12:49–53.**

After His parable, Jesus gave harsh but necessary warnings. He *will* come back again, and He promised that His rule and reign include judgment, which is often symbolized by fire (12:49). Jesus knew He would endure God's judgment too—in His death, when He carried the sins of God's kids and bore God's wrath on their behalf.

In the death and resurrection of Jesus, we're confronted with His divinity. Jesus came to bring salvation, but in doing so, He also became the great divider of humanity—the line of demarcation between life and death. In the ancient Near East, where familial ties were a person's primary identity marker, His statement about divided families would've been shocking. Families will fall on both sides of the line. It's a devastating truth, but it's a truth nonetheless. Ultimately, as disciples, our allegiance resides first and foremost with Christ.

6. Do you have family members who have decided not to follow Jesus? Write a short prayer for them below, asking God to open their hearts to the truth.

7. **Review 12:54–59.**

Jesus gave two brief, final warnings in today's reading, and they're directed at the broader crowd, not just the disciples. First, He warned them to pay attention to the more important things in life, such as the Messianic signs He was showing them. Second, He warned them to live righteously— otherwise, punishment would come for them. In this parable, He used examples of earthly judgment, but in context, He was almost certainly pointing to eternal judgment. Even in parables, Jesus didn't dilute His message: He is the only path to eternal freedom and joy, and those who believe His words will follow Him on the path of righteousness.

8. What is one thing you'd change if you knew Jesus was coming back in your lifetime?

Luke 13:1–21

 **READ LUKE 13:1–21**

Today's reading opens with two stories about mass casualties, and not much is known about either account.

1. Review 13:1–5.

At the time, Pilate was appointed as a Roman governor over the area of Judea. A group of Galileans went to Jerusalem to offer sacrifices—like all the Jews did three times every year—and Pilate had them killed. A common thought in the day was that punishment and suffering were always the result of sin. So Jesus asked if they thought those particular Galileans were killed because they were worse than other Galileans.

Before they could respond, Jesus answered His own question with a no, but acknowledged in the same breath that judgment would come for all unless they repented. He presented two options: repentance and judgment.

Next, He discussed a tower in Siloam that had fallen over and killed eighteen people. Jesus made the point again that the severity of one's suffering is not linked to the severity of one's sin.

2. Using your favorite study tool, find an example of a righteous person in Scripture who endured suffering. How can this person's story encourage you when you suffer?

It can be challenging to discern why hard things are happening in our lives. Jesus warned that regardless of how we live, everyone will experience final, eternal judgment, and He called the people again to repent and turn to God. Those who turn to God will be judged by *Christ's* righteousness, not our own.

In this life, God's kids will certainly face discipline (Hebrews 12:6), and we will often face the natural consequences of our choices, but discipline and consequence are altogether different from judgment and punishment. Those who have been adopted into God's family through the saving work of Jesus will *never, ever, ever* see God's wrath. Jesus took on all the Father's wrath for our sins when He died on the cross (1 Thessalonians 1:10, 5:9–10; John 3:36).

3. Match the reference below with the truth it proclaims:

Romans 4:5	In Christ, we become the righteousness of God.
Romans 5:19	Christ became our righteousness and sanctification.
Romans 10:4	Christ is the end of the law for righteousness to those who believe.
1 Corinthians 1:30	Christ became our righteousness and sanctification. Christ's righteousness made many righteous.
2 Corinthians 5:21	God justifies the ungodly, whose faith is counted as righteousness.

4. **Review 13:6–9.**

Jesus segued into a parable as He continued His call to repentance. A man planted a fig tree in his vineyard and had a vinedresser tend to it. In a span of three years, it hadn't produced fruit. The man was ready to chop it down, but the gardener asked for one more year of tending, watering, and fertilizing before giving up on it.

5. Match the characters in the parable with who you think they represent.

This was almost certainly a metaphor for Israel. Not only had Israel often been compared to a fig tree in Scripture (Hosea 9:10, Jeremiah 8:13, Jeremiah 24), but Jesus spent three years ministering to them, and Israel was still lost in their ways. The consequence for not bearing fruit was severe, but Jesus was merciful and patient with Israel, just as He is merciful and patient with us.

6. If this was a parable about Israel's fruitlessness, what kind of "fruit" do you think the gardener was hoping it would bear? **(For help, see 3:8–9 and 6:43–44.)**

7. What does this parable reveal about God's heart?

8. **Review 13:10–17.**

Luke transitions out of his long section on warnings, repentance, and judgment and takes us into a beautiful story of Jesus healing a woman.

9. Fill in the chart below.

What physical symptom did the woman display?	
What caused the physical symptom?	
How long had the woman been impacted?	
How long did it take for her to recover?	

This story is not without drama. The ruler of the synagogue found out about this healing and chided Jesus for working on the Sabbath.

10. In your own words, summarize Jesus's response and logic.

11. **Review 13:18–21.**

In our final section, Jesus painted two pictures of the kingdom of God. We've already learned about one of those things: leaven. A little leaven impacts an entire loaf. Likewise, a mustard seed was one of the smallest seeds known to Jesus's audience, but when watered and tended, the tree can grow to roughly twenty feet tall and wide!

The Jews thought the Messiah would come with triumphant power to overrule Rome and set them free, but Jesus's ministry was like a mustard seed—something seemingly "insignificant" that would grow beyond their comprehension. And just as He promised, the kingdom has continued to expand, reaching across thousands of years to change our hearts and lives today!

Luke 13:22–35

✝ **READ LUKE 13:22-35**

In today's reading, Luke said Jesus was "journeying toward Jerusalem" (13:22). Though Luke doesn't record events chronologically, it's worth noting that the journey to Jerusalem marked the final weeks of Jesus's life. He was heading to Jerusalem to die. Any time we read about that part of the timeline, we see Him reiterating His call to repentance more emphatically.

1. **Review 13:22–30.**

Someone who encountered Jesus asked Him how many people would be saved. If you have a question about salvation, the Savior is the right one to ask! But there are two things worth noting about the man's question. First, the question was general, not personal. He didn't ask, "Will *I* be saved?" Second, we don't know what the man was referring to specifically—saved from what? It's likely he was referring to being saved from the oppression of Rome, because few people Jesus encountered had a lens to understand the kingdom—they primarily thought about temporary things, not eternal things.

Per usual, Jesus didn't answer the question being asked—He gave information that was even more important. First, He made the answer personal.

2. What did Jesus encourage the man to do in 13:24? Summarize His answer in your own words.

3. According to 13:26–27, why did the person in Jesus's illustration think he belonged in the kingdom? Why was he turned away?

Jesus wasn't saying He *wanted* there to be only a few who would come to trust Him—He was acknowledging that many would refuse. There'll be a time when those He doesn't know will be shut out. The narrow door becomes a closed door at some point. For each person, there's an urgency to not just listen to the words of Jesus, but actually respond.

Second, Jesus spoke about the kingdom in His reply, pointing to a salvation that was far greater than any earthly salvation.

4. In 13:29, where did Jesus say the people in the kingdom would come from? What was He implying?

Jesus showed that people from all over the world would be included in God's kingdom. It wasn't about nationality or ethnicity—it was about knowing Him personally and putting your faith in Him. Being of Gentile descent doesn't mean exclusion, and being of Jewish descent doesn't automatically mean inclusion. He also pointed out the last will be first and the first will be last. In other words, status and power hold no weight in the kingdom of God. Everyone is presented with the same opportunity to know and trust Jesus.

5. Have you ever been tempted to elevate yourself—even in your own mind—because of the faith of your ancestors (13:28), your ethnicity (13:29–30), or even your church attendance (13:26)? How does the message of Jesus put those thoughts in their proper place?

6. **Review 13:31–35.**

Even though Jesus spoke harshly against the Pharisees as a whole, there were some who had an amicable relationship with Him (see 7:36). As He taught, a group of Pharisees came to warn Him that Herod was plotting to kill Him. Jesus knew this, of course, and basically responded with, "Tell him I've got a job to do, and I'm making sure it gets done."

Then Jesus lamented over Jerusalem—this city had been set apart by God as the center of worship for Israel, but it had become one of the most unsafe places for a true prophet of God.

7. **Using a study tool, research what event Jesus was referring to in 13:35.** Has it already happened or are we still waiting for it to happen?

Jesus mourned over Jerusalem, longing to gather and protect its people. But He said there'd be a day when they call Him "blessed," prophesying about His triumphal entry into Jerusalem, which happened on Palm Sunday, not long after this conversation took place.

Even on the journey to His own execution, He urged His followers to repent and put their faith in Him. He spoke with urgency and purpose as He made His way to the cross. Thankfully, the narrow door is still open.

Luke 14

 **READ LUKE 14**

1. **Review 14:1–6.**

Today isn't our first time encountering Jesus healing on the Sabbath (4:31–37, 6:6–11, 13:10–17). The other Sabbath healings Luke recorded took place in synagogues; but this time, Jesus healed in the home of a Pharisee—so you can bet they were keeping a close eye on Him! Because a man with dropsy was seated in front of Him, many scholars believe this man had been planted by the Pharisees in an effort to trap Jesus. It's fascinating to think they may have fully expected Him to do the miraculous yet still refused to believe in Him. Signs and wonders don't change hard hearts.

There was no command not to heal on the Sabbath, but as we've noted before, the Pharisees added their own traditions to God's laws. Jesus loved to jump the "fence" the Pharisees had set up around God's commands— not out of arrogance, but because the Pharisees' fences were misrepresenting God's heart and oppressing the people. Imagine the callousness that denies a hurting person healing based on the day of the week!

2. What is *dropsy*? **Do a web search and write the definition below.**

Knowing He was being watched, Jesus posed a question to the lawyers and Pharisees. He wasn't looking for the answer but was using the question to show their hypocrisy. And just like we saw with a Sabbath healing earlier this week (13:10–17), the Pharisees didn't have an answer. Jesus addressed the problem with their hearts and minds—their lack of both logic and compassion—healed the man, and sent him on his way. Unlike many healing accounts, the text never mentions the man asking to be healed or worshiping Jesus in response.

3. What do you think: Was the man a plant by the Pharisees? How would you feel if you were used as part of their plot against a Man who healed you?

4. **Review 14:7–11.**

After this experience, Jesus apparently had a captive audience. He began telling the guests at the Pharisee's dinner party parables about parties. The first was about a wedding feast. The seating arrangements revealed prestige and honor. The most important, honored guest had a particular seat at the table. The wisdom of Jesus says not to assume your own status, but to be humble and assume the lowest rank.

5. In your own words, summarize the message of this parable.

6. As a reminder, who had been seated across from Jesus at the party?

7. **Review 14:12–14.**

Next, He turned to His host and described a great banquet. He painted a picture of welcoming the outcasts—those who have nothing to offer you in return. In this imagery, Jesus showed us a picture of the heart of God and gave the opportunity to demonstrate that kind of love to others. He said that was the path to being truly blessed.

As He was speaking, someone at the table interjected: "Blessed is every-one who will eat bread in the kingdom of God!" (v. 15). Perhaps this was an attempted rebuttal, because Luke records Jesus's counterpoint about the kingdom. He said the poor are the ones who really understand the kingdom and get the blessing of it.

8. **Review 14:15–24.** Fill in the chart below regarding the three reasons the rich invitees gave for missing the banquet.

Verse	Invitee's Excuse
14:18	
14:19	
14:20	

9. How would you summarize all three responses?

Often the poor don't have the same distractions as the rich, but the busy lives of the rich and well-known overtake right priorities. All of these excuses—land, possessions, and relational blessing—are blessings. But those temporary blessings become a problem when they take precedence over the eternal things. When God's good gifts distract us from the Giver (James 1:17), we've lost our way.

10. **Read Mark 4:18–19.** In this portion from the parable of the four soils, what chokes out the growth of this particular seed? What distracts you the most from time with God?

11. What did the master long for in Luke 14:23? What does this reveal about the heart of God?

12. **Review 14:25–33.** Is there something you've had to give up to truly devote yourself to Jesus? What was that experience like for you? Do you believe He is worthy of the cost?

As disciples of Christ, if we aren't using our new status as children of God to be salt in the world—preserving, purifying, enhancing—Jesus says it's worthless. While some of His language may be hyperbolic to drive home the point, it's also clarifying. When we understand the overwhelming goodness of being invited into the kingdom of God, we can't help but risk it all and share with others what walking with Him is like—because He's where the joy is!

13. What stood out to you most in this week's study? Why?

14. What did you learn or relearn about God and His character this week?

Corresponding Psalm & Prayer

✝ READ PSALM 147

1. What correlation do you see between Psalm 147 and this week's study of Jesus as Savior?

2. What portions of this psalm stand out to you most?

3. Close by praying this prayer aloud:

Father,
   You know the exact number of stars in the sky; You put them there! You make rain for the grass to grow and provide food for all

creatures to eat. Your power and wisdom are greater than we could ever understand, yet Your heart is for the vulnerable. You heal the brokenhearted and lift up the humble. It's good and fitting to praise You, and I do!

I confess that I've had an unhealthy fear of other people and their opinions instead of a healthy fear of You. I haven't believed Your Son, who said that it's Your good pleasure to give us the kingdom. I've built bigger barns to hoard my resources—or wanted to—instead of building bigger tables to share my blessings and my faith.

Please give me the courage to live my faith out loud. Give me the faith I need to put my resources—my time and energy and money and hope—into things that matter. Show me how to spend my time preparing eagerly and joyfully for Your return. Return, Lord.

I surrender my life to You, Lord—every moment of my day, each decision I make, I yield my will and way to Your perfect will and way.

I love You too. Amen.

Rest, Catch Up, or Dig Deeper

WEEKLY CHALLENGE

On Day 1, we asked, "If someone were to randomly poll a handful of people in your life and ask them about your relationship with Jesus, what would they say?" So we're going to actually do that! Have conversations with three people in your life and ask them to describe what they know about your relationship with Jesus. One should be a close friend or relative, one should be an acquaintance, and one should be a non-Christian friend or relative. Aim to not be defensive or angry. Just listen and learn, and do your best to be loving to the other person. Take notes on what they say and plan to learn from this experience.

Luke 15–17:

The Illustrations of the Savior

DAILY BIBLE READING

Day 1. Luke 15

Day 2. Luke 16:1–18

Day 3. Luke 16:19–31

Day 4. Luke 17:1–10

Day 5. Luke 17:11–37

Day 6. Psalm 103

Day 7. Catch-Up Day

Corresponds to Days 300–301 of *The Bible Recap*.

WEEKLY CHALLENGE

See page 205 for more information.

Luke 15

READ LUKE 15

Some theologians refer to Luke 15 as the Gospel of the Outcasts, while others call the chapter the Parables of Joy. As you learn about each of the three parables, two of which appear only in Luke, note that the high point of each story isn't just the homecoming of what was lost, but the rejoicing over it.

1. **Review 15:1–7.**

While the "tax collectors and sinners" (15:1) continued to draw near to Jesus, the Pharisees and scribes spent their time grumbling about Jesus's company. Sound familiar? The people who knew they were sinners also knew they needed Jesus, and because Jesus found them, their lives were changed. So when Jesus heard the Pharisees' same old complaints, He told them three parables about the lost being found.

In the first parable, a sheep was lost from the rest of his flock. When the shepherd left the flock in the open country, there would have been other shepherds to look after them. He wasn't recklessly abandoning 99 percent of his sheep to track down the missing 1 percent. He was ensuring all his sheep were cared for while finding the one who was lost. God's love for us is both collective and individual.

When the shepherd found the lost sheep, it might've been injured or exhausted. Or maybe the shepherd just needed to remind the sheep it was cared for. Whatever the reason, the shepherd picked up the sheep and carried it back.

2. Fill in the blanks in Jesus's words from 15:7.

Just so, I tell you, there will be more joy in heaven over one _____ who _____ than over ninety-nine _____ _____ who _____ _____ _____.

Jesus spoke with irony, addressing the Pharisees. They didn't believe they were sick (5:31) or blind (6:39), and they didn't believe they were sinners. There is only one person who has ever lived who needed no repentance, and He welcomes repentant sinners with rejoicing.

Then Jesus told a story about a lost coin and the woman who searched tirelessly to find it.

3. **Review 15:8–10.** What did the woman do when she found the coin? How is that similar to what happens when a sinner repents?

4. **Review 15:11–16.**

If you've already heard or read the third parable in today's Scripture passage, you've heard the younger son referred to as "prodigal." But Jesus never called him that. Jesus described what the son did; He didn't name him based on his sins.

5. What did the younger son do? **Now look up the word** *prodigal* **in a dictionary.** What are the two primary definitions?

6. **Review 15:17–24.**

When the son was returning home, his father, who must have been looking for him, spotted him from "a long way off." The father did something undignified by his culture's standards: He *ran* to his son. As the son recited the speech he'd prepared at rock bottom, his father interrupted him. But he didn't lecture him or tell him how much he'd been hurt; he celebrated because his lost son was found. The son repented and returned, and his father rejoiced.

The younger son was certainly lost. He had demanded his inheritance early, left his responsibilities behind, and squandered his father's generosity. But what if the older son was lost too?

7. **Review 15:25–32.** What did the older son say about himself? What did he say about his father? What did he say about his brother?

What the Older Brother Said . . .

About Himself	About His Father	About His Brother

When the oldest son found out what the commotion was about, he was appalled. He reminded the father of his own flawless track record. He assumed the worst about where his brother had been and who he'd spent his time with. He refused to even claim his brother as a relative, calling him "this son of yours." He was so caught up in his own entitlement that he was blind to the miracle of redemption.

8. In the chart below, note evidence for how each of the father's sons is lost.

Son	Evidence	Scripture Reference(s)
Younger		
Older		

It seems the older son was a prodigal too—wasting the father's generosity. And in his own way, the father meets the definition of a prodigal—extravagantly lavishing love on both of his undeserving children.

If you've ever read these parables and thought to yourself, *It's just one sheep* or *He made his choice*, you probably identify with the older son. You've been in the field, working diligently, all along. No one threw you a party for the tireless days you toiled in the hot sun.

But when we come to ourselves, we understand that even though we may *feel* like the older son, we're also the younger son: prodigals wasting our Father's goodness, in need of a Savior who finds us, welcomes us, and *celebrates* us. On the other side of repentance is restoration and rejoicing.

9. Is there something in your life that you're afraid to repent of? Is there a person you could contact who would rejoice with you over your repentance and restoration?

Luke 16:1–18

┬ READ LUKE 16:1-18

Today we read one of the most difficult to interpret parables in Luke, if not all of the Gospels. So as a reminder, parables usually teach one main lesson. We aren't meant to create multiple levels of meaning here or identify direct parallels for each character and event in the story. Don't attempt to; you'll only leave yourself confused and frustrated.

1. **Review 16:1–9.**

In the parable, a rich man found out that his manager was mismanaging his wealth. When the rich man confronted him, the manager didn't even try to defend himself. He was guilty. The manager knew that after his dismissal, his money would soon run out. And that's when his shrewdness kicked in.

2. **Do a web search to find some synonyms for shrewd.** Write down two synonyms with a negative connotation and two with a positive connotation.

3. How did the rich man react to his soon-to-be-former manager's shrewd actions?

    A. He was angry that the manager cheated him out of more money.

    B. He was impressed with the manager's clever thinking.

    C. He was grateful that the manager finally did his job.

Then Jesus told His disciples the point of His parable: "For the sons of this world are more shrewd in dealing with their own generation than the sons of light" (16:8). The worldly were wiser with earthly matters than the disciples were with eternal matters. Jesus wanted them to fix their eyes on eternity.

4. **Now read 16:9 in the NLT below.** Then summarize Jesus's lesson to His disciples.

> "Here's the lesson: Use your worldly resources to benefit others and make friends. Then, when your possessions are gone, they will welcome you to an eternal home."

5. **Review 16:10–13.**

Money isn't always—but can be—an idol. We cannot simultaneously serve money and serve God. Everything we have is from Him and belongs to Him. When we are generous with what He's given us, no matter how much or how little we have, we use money to serve God. We can't use money to buy our way into God's kingdom, but we *can* use it to show glimpses of the kingdom here on earth.

6. How does generosity help you trust God more? How can earthly investments make an eternal impact?

7. **Review 16:14–17.** Who overheard the parable of the dishonest manager? How did they respond?

Jesus was teaching His disciples, but of course He knew that His audience included His critics. The Pharisees thought their money was a sign that God was pleased with them, even though they got the money by oppressing the vulnerable (Matthew 23). Even so, when they heard Jesus's words, they ridiculed Him.

8. **Look up 16:15 in a few different Bible translations.** In your own words, summarize what Jesus said to the Pharisees.

The Pharisees often quoted Scripture at Jesus, falsely accusing Him of breaking one law or the other. But Jesus told them He wasn't there to throw the entire old system into the trash. He didn't void the law; He fulfilled it.

9. **Read 16:16 in the NLT below.** What was JTB ushering in?

> Until John the Baptist, the law of Moses and the messages of the prophets were your guides. But now the Good News of the Kingdom of God is preached, and everyone is eager to get in.

Even though the Pharisees refused to believe it, the Savior who God's people had been longing for since the beginning of time was here. He brought with Him good news about God's kingdom. He fulfilled the Old Testament prophecies *and* He fulfilled the law.

10. **Look up the following passages.** Then draw a line matching each prophecy or law to how Jesus fulfilled it.

Scripture	How Jesus Fulfilled It
Exodus 12:1–11	He was David's descendant who would reign forever.
2 Samuel 7:12–13	He was the sacrifice who atoned for our sin.
Leviticus 16:29–34	He was the Passover Lamb.

11. Write a prayer of thankfulness for the ways in which Jesus fulfilled the law and prophets.

12. **Review 16:18.**

To illustrate His point about not voiding the law, Jesus gave an example of what honoring the law looks like. Moses gave the Israelites God's permission for divorce (Deuteronomy 24:1–4). There were complicated situational examples in Moses's instructions, but in Luke's account, Jesus pointed to marriage as a holy example of how the law wasn't passing away.

Jesus leveled up the law. He never diminished or subtracted from it. When He spoke of the law, He raised the standard and pointed to the state of our hearts. None of us have ever kept the law perfectly. Praise God for giving us a Savior who kept the law in our place!

DAY 3

Luke 16:19–31

 READ LUKE 16:19-31

Remember that Jesus had been teaching His disciples when the Pharisees interrupted Him. He began addressing them directly, which is where we picked up today. Jesus continued talking to the Pharisees, wrapping up His theme on how we use our money and resources here on earth.

The story He told them is often referred to as a parable, but it doesn't quite fit the qualifications. Most notably, some of the main characters are named. So it's possible this wasn't a parable, but rather a story about real people and real events.

Jesus set up a vivid scene of a wealthy man wearing luxurious clothes and eating rich food, while another man lay destitute outside of his gate. He had so little strength left in his diseased body that he couldn't even fight away the street dogs who treated his open sores like food. Finally, relief came for the poor man.

1. What happened to Lazarus after his death?

The Pharisees would've believed that being by Abraham's side was the best possible eternal destination. So it would've been unsettling for them that this poor man (who they assumed sinned his way into his suffering state) was positioned in this esteemed spot after his death. Even more unsettling was that the rich man—the person in Jesus's story with whom the Pharisees most identified—had a different destination.

2. **Using Hebrew and Greek dictionaries, define the words below:**

- Sheol (Hebrew)—

- Hades (Greek)—

In the two main original languages of the Bible, these words have similar meanings: an after-death destination. Both Lazarus and the rich man were aware of their locations after their deaths, just as both believers and nonbelievers will have an understanding of their eternity, whether it's one of blessing or suffering.

3. Fill in the chart below according to 16:25.

Person	What did they receive in life?		What did they receive after death?
Rich Man			
		"...but *now*..."	
Lazarus			

There is a great chasm once we reach our eternal destination. When we die, there isn't a waiting room. There isn't an opportunity for a second chance. There is only eternity. In light of this, the rich man wanted to warn his brothers against having his same fate. He thought they'd believe the truth from a man who'd risen from the dead, but Abraham knew better.

4. In 16:31, why did Abraham deny the rich man's request?

We have a Savior who rose from the dead, and yet there were—and still are—unbelievers. Not even a biology-defying, history-altering miracle softens the hardest of hearts. They won't be convinced, but they reject Christ at their own peril.

5. **Read John 3:36 below and fill in the blanks.**

Whoever _____ in the Son has eternal _____; whoever does not obey the Son shall _____ see life, but the _____ _____ _____ remains on him.

As we've talked about, generosity and good works aren't requirements for eternal life. But they are hallmarks of a changed heart. The rich man wasn't condemned on account of his wealth—after all, Abraham was rich, having hundreds of servants in his household, but Lazarus met him in heaven. The rich man was condemned because of his unrepentant heart. Jesus's urgent warning to the unrepentant Pharisees was clear: Repent, believe, and live out your faith. But their hearts were hard.

6. Did anything in today's reading challenge your thoughts on the afterlife?

Luke 17:1–10

 READ LUKE 17:1-10

As we've seen previously in Luke, today's topics are most likely sequenced thematically rather than chronologically. As you study today's three topics, challenge yourself to find a connecting theme.

1. **Review 17:1–4.** Who was Jesus talking to? Who was Jesus talking about?

By teaching their followers their ways, the Pharisees were perpetuating a corrupt system of leadership, ensuring that the vulnerable would continue to be ignored or abused. Teachers and leaders have an extra measure of responsibility in God's kingdom.

2. **Read James 3:1.** What warning does James give to teachers?

Jesus went further in His warning, illustrating His point with an example His listeners would've been familiar with. A millstone was used for grinding, and depending on what was being ground, it could weigh anywhere from hundreds to thousands of pounds. It was so heavy that it was turned by a donkey or oxen walking in circles around a track. All of that to say, Jesus wasn't talking about a small rock here. He said tying that giant stone around your neck and being thrown into the sea was better than being the cause of a new believer's sin.

Then Jesus gave His disciples a short and powerful exhortation.

3. Write the first four words of 17:3 in the ESV. What did Jesus tell His disciples to do before He gave instructions on rebuking a brother? Why do you think He did that?

A rebuke is a sharp charge of disapproval. Unlike what many people *claim* to be doing on social media comment threads, a rebuke is *not* a chance to humiliate another image bearer. It's an attempt to call someone to repentance—turning 180 degrees away from sin and toward God—in hopeful anticipation of a restored fellowship with God and fellow believers.

4. Fill in the flowchart according to 17:3.

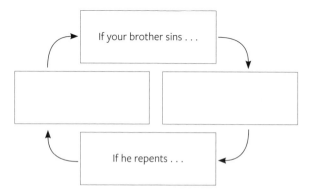

If your brother sins . . .

If he repents . . .

Rebuke must be tied to your own willingness to forgive, and the right response to repentance is forgiveness. Jesus said that if that person repents, we *must* forgive them. For that to happen, we have to carry in our hearts the willingness, and even the desire, to forgive them. Forgiveness doesn't mean automatic reconciliation or relational restoration, but it does start the journey down that road. God alone softens our hearts and gives us the capacity for forgiveness, even when we've been sinned against. And He alone gives us the capacity to righteously rebuke someone while simultaneously preparing for the opportunity to humbly forgive them.

5. **Review 17:5–6.** How did the apostles respond to Jesus's teaching?

Jesus assured the disciples that it's not the *size* of their faith that matters most; it's the *object* in which their faith is placed (see John 15:7). Even a tiny amount of rightly placed faith can have extraordinary results. It's the quality of the faith's source, not the quantity of the faith itself.

6. Have you seen a great amount of wrongly placed faith (either yours or someone else's) lead to heartbreak?

7. **Review 17:7–10.**

Jesus then taught about the duty of servants. It's important to remember that not everything in the Bible is *prescriptive*; sometimes it's *descriptive*. Meaning, sometimes it tells us what we should do, and other times it tells us the reality of what is happening. Jesus wasn't condoning servitude, but rather painting a picture His disciples would have easily understood: a servant completing his duties.

8. Using a Greek lexicon, look up *achreios*, the word used for how the servants should describe themselves (17:10). What does it mean?

Most English Bible translations translate the word as "unworthy," which is a better picture of the meaning here than "unprofitable." Despite what social media gurus may say, we are indeed unworthy servants. For instance, 1 Corinthians 4:7 asks, "What do you have that you did not receive?" God owes us nothing, yet He's given us everything we have. We're unworthy of His love, yet He has lavished it upon us nonetheless. God never calls us to think *poorly* of ourselves but to think *rightly* of ourselves. When we have a right view of ourselves and of God's abundant love, it moves our hearts toward humility and worship!

9. In the words of Jesus, pay attention to yourself. Write out a prayer confessing how you've been an unworthy servant. Ask Him to show you how to let go of what you think you deserve.

Luke 17:11–37

READ LUKE 17:11–37

1. **Review 17:11–19.** Where was Jesus going?

2. **Review 9:51 and 13:22.** What do you notice?

We've read this before, but because Luke's record isn't chronological, we're covering it again. In the final weeks of His life, Jesus made His way back to Jerusalem, which was so much more than a physical destination. He went there to suffer. To die. To be buried. To rise again. To bear the wrath for the sins of all of humanity and offer life everlasting to all who would believe. In Jerusalem, our Savior changed the entire course of human history.

On His way there, He encountered ten lepers. They stayed at a distance, raising their voices to ask for help.

3. Fill in the chart below according to 17:14.

What Jesus Said	What the Lepers Did

All ten of the lepers demonstrated faith. They obeyed Jesus *before* they were healed, walking to show themselves to the priests before the leprosy was even gone. But only one demonstrated gratitude.

4. What did one leper do differently?

Earlier in the gospel of Luke, Jesus told this story: "And there were many lepers in Israel in the time of the prophet Elisha, and none of them was cleansed, but only Naaman the Syrian" (4:27). God's people had rejected the prophet Elisha, so Elisha healed Naaman, who was, notably, a Gentile. Like Elisha, Jesus—the Prophet who *fulfilled* prophecy—also encountered many lepers. Here, unlike Elisha, He healed them all. He knew that only one of them would come back to praise Him, and still, He gave all of them the gift of health. All ten were cleansed. But only one of them was *made well*. The Samaritan's healing wasn't just physical; it was eternal.

5. In a Greek lexicon, look up *healed* (17:15) and *made well* (17:19). What do you notice?

Those of us who are Gentile Christians are the Samaritan leper. We were rotting away from the disease of our own sin, but Jesus made us well. Gratitude is the right response to all that God gives us. And genuine gratitude leads to praise.

6. Write a prayer of thanksgiving and praise to God for healing you physically or for making you well spiritually.

7. **Review 17:20–37.**

The Pharisees were back, and they asked Jesus when the kingdom of God would come. They were looking for signs and wonders that would mark the dramatic arrival of a great political or military leader to free them from Rome's oppression.

8. Fill in the blanks from 17:21.

> For behold, the kingdom of God is ___ ___ _____ ___ _____.

Instead of "in the midst of you," some Bible translations say "within you." While that's an accurate literal translation of the Greek word, the meaning is confusing in English. Jesus wasn't telling the Pharisees that they had the Holy Spirit. (And He certainly wasn't telling them that they were gods, as some twist His words to say.) He was telling them that He was right there, among them, revealing the kingdom of God. But they refused to see it.

9. Jesus explained that the kingdom of God would arrive as people lived their normal lives. What are the two Old Testament examples of this that He gave?

- 17:27—

- 17:28–29—

10. What are the two universal examples of this Jesus gave in 17:31?

- _____

- _____

The Pharisees asked Jesus when the kingdom was coming. Then the disciples asked where it would come. As He often did, Jesus answered neither question, but also both.

11. **Look up 17:37 in a study Bible or commentary.** What did Jesus mean about the corpse and the vultures?

The kingdom of God has come, and is coming. The kingdom of God is here, and there. Don't spend your days looking for signs or a timeline. Spend your days preparing your heart—in prayer, in the Word, in sharing the good news with others. He's coming again, and for those who know Him, eternal glory awaits! He's where the joy is!

12. What stood out to you most in this week's study? Why?

13. What did you learn or relearn about God and His character this week?

Corresponding Psalm & Prayer

READ PSALM 103

1. What correlation do you see between Psalm 103 and this week's study of Jesus as Savior?

2. What portions of this psalm stand out to you most?

3. Close by praying this prayer aloud:

Father,
You forgive, heal, redeem, and satisfy me. You're so patient with me. You crown me with steadfast love and mercy. It's right for me to bless Your name and tell others about Your goodness!

Like the younger son in the parable, I've wasted Your abundant generosity. And like the older son, I've let my angry entitlement blind me to the miracle of mercy. Like the father did for both his sons, and like You did for David, show me Your compassion.

I've rebuked others with no intention to forgive them. I've seen my neighbors in need without even pausing to pray for them. I've withheld compassion and generosity. Forgive me, Lord.

I am Your unworthy servant. Teach me how to obey You out of humble awe, rather than begrudging obligation. Give me opportunities to show compassion to my neighbors just like You've done for me. Show me how You want me to invest the resources You've given me here on earth. Remind me—as many times as needed—that it's all Yours, anyway.

I surrender my life to You, Lord—every moment of my day, each decision I make, I yield my will and way to Your perfect will and way.

I love You too. Amen.

Rest, Catch Up, or Dig Deeper

WEEKLY CHALLENGE

A recurring theme in Luke 16–17 is the value of showing the kingdom of God in practical and faithful ways. From donations to ministries and missionaries, to volunteer hours at a local shelter, every small act of practically living out our faith demonstrates a right view of God and what He's given us. This week, pray for God's guidance in making an earthly investment—time or money—with the potential for eternal impact.

Luke 18–20:

The Character
of the Savior

DAILY BIBLE READING

Day 1. Luke 18

Day 2. Luke 19:1–27

Day 3. Luke 19:28–48

Day 4. Luke 20:1–26

Day 5. Luke 20:27–47

Day 6. Psalm 81

Day 7. Catch-Up Day

Corresponds to Days 303, 306, and 309 of *The Bible Recap*.

WEEKLY CHALLENGE

See page 230 for more information.

Luke 18

🕆 READ LUKE 18

Jesus continued teaching the crowd, using one of His favorite methods: parables. We may be tempted to make a dozen different meanings or analogies out of these symbolic stories, but it's important to keep context in mind to understand what Jesus actually meant.

1. **Review 18:1–8.** What main point was Jesus communicating?

    A. God is a righteous judge.

    B. We irritate God with our many requests.

    C. God wants us to talk to Him about our desires.

    D. God is reluctant to respond to our prayers.

In this story, the woman had to overcome the worldly judge's reluctance to help her. In the same way, we might feel weary in prayer and be tempted to believe the lie that God is unwilling to answer our pleas. When we think like this, we miss the point of the story altogether.

2. Using the options below, compare the judge's character to God's character. Underline the characteristics of the judge. Circle the characteristics of God.

Unfair

Loves to answer requests for people's good

Fair

No interest in the widow

Deep love for His kids

Answered the request out of self-interest

Jesus gave instructions to pray persistently. He prayed "saying the same words" (Mark 14:39), and Paul prayed a repeated prayer (2 Corinthians 12:8). God isn't bothered by our repetitive asking. Be careful not to believe the lie that you're a bother to your Savior.

3. **Review 18:9–14.**

In the next parable, Jesus addressed our heart posture as we pray. He wants us to make our requests known to Him (Philippians 4:6), and He also cares about our motives when we do. The Pharisee relied on his status and his good deeds, while the tax collector recognized his desperate need for God. "Everyone who exalts himself will be humbled, but the one who humbles himself will be exalted" (18:14). This concept of humble asking is repeated throughout Scripture.

4. **Look up the verses below and fill in the chart.**

Verse	Who said it?	What did they say?
Proverbs 3:34		
1 Peter 5:6		
James 4:6		

5. Take a moment to assess your heart posture when you pray. Do you feel like you deserve a yes from God because of your good works? Are you desperate for His will to be done? Use Scripture to support your answer.

6. **Review 18:15–17.**

In Jesus's day, it was customary for moms to bring their one-year-old babies to a rabbi (a teacher) to receive a blessing. On this day, a moms' group showed up with their little ones so they could get a blessing from Jesus. The disciples rebuked them, but Jesus told the parents to come forward and corrected the crowds for their heart posture.

7. Write out Jesus's words from 18:16–17.

On our own, we bring nothing to God to gain our salvation. We're as dependent on Jesus as diapered toddlers crying out to be changed. In our childlikeness, we may not even fully understand His words, but we're impacted by His touch. Jesus says we must be humble and dependent to enter His kingdom.

8. What challenges cause you to realize your need for Jesus? In what areas are you tempted to forsake childlikeness and a dependent posture before God?

9. **Review 18:18–30.**

Upon hearing these words, a rich man with authority asked what he could do to earn eternal life. It's easy to make a claim that God hates money, and some have taught that it's more righteous to be poor than wealthy, but neither are true. God hates it when we love our money more than Him (1 Timothy 6:9–10). He saw the heart posture of the rich ruler and challenged him to let go of the one thing he was holding with a clenched fist. Abraham, David, Zacchaeus, and Joseph of Arimathea are just a handful of the rich men mentioned in Scripture who chose to put God first in spite of their wealth. Jesus wrapped up the conversation by telling them that those who hold earthly priorities more loosely than kingdom priorities will be rewarded both now *and* throughout eternity. When we live openhandedly, we can have our best life with Him now and an even better life with Him forever!

10. Is there anything you feel like God is prompting you to release from your grip? If so, what is it? And what steps of obedience and accountability can you take in this area?

11. **Review 18:31–43.**

After this, Jesus and the twelve walked on their own, and He told them, for the third time, that He would be treated poorly and killed and would rise to life on the third day. They listened with both ears, but they didn't have the eyes to see the full picture. As Jesus continued walking among His spiritually blind disciples, they met a man who was physically blind and desperate for healing. Only God can give us the spiritual eyes to understand His heart, and only He has the power to heal physical ailments with a word.

12. **Revisit 18:42 and 17:5.** How does your faith impact your prayers? Write out two seemingly impossible prayer requests—perhaps including a prayer for spiritual growth and a prayer for a physical need or a personal desire to be met. As you pray, ask God to increase your faith.

Luke 19:1–27

 **READ LUKE 19:1–27**

1. **Review 19:1–10.**

Zacchaeus knew Jesus was in town, and he was determined to see the One with a reputation for being a friend to sinners and tax collectors. Zacchaeus might've desired a friend or he might've been curious about the Messiah. We know by his actions that he was desperate to encounter Jesus. He ran to get ahead of the crowd and because of his small stature, he climbed a tree to be able to see. Pulling up one's robe and running was considered a shameful act in this culture. Today, it would be like a grown man running down the street wearing only boxers. It seems like Zacchaeus wasn't thinking about his status or his reputation; he was only thinking about a potential encounter with the Savior.

2. How did Jesus address Zacchaeus in 19:5? Why might that be noteworthy or significant? Use a Bible dictionary or other resource to look up the meaning of the name Zacchaeus.

Jesus didn't say, "Hey, short guy!" or "Hey, you, in the tree!" Instead, He called the chief tax collector by name. It's possible they'd never even met before, which adds to the intrigue. Jesus knew the importance of a name, and John 10:3 says He calls His sheep by their name and leads them. Jesus called out, "Zacchaeus!" which means "pure, innocent one," a name likely given by his parents and a name he hadn't lived up to as he spent his adult life deceiving people and dealing corruptly with money.

3. Fill in the blanks from 19:6, 8.

> [Zacchaeus] _____ and came down and received [Jesus]
> _____. . . . Zacchaeus stood and said to the Lord, "Behold, Lord,
> _____ _____ of my goods I give to the poor. And if I have defrauded
> anyone of anything, I _____ it _____."

Zacchaeus ran to Jesus joyfully. In front of a grumbling crowd, the tax collector announced that money wasn't the king of his life and that he'd quadruply repay anything he had taken wrongly. With a repentant heart, he began walking in the identity of his given name: pure, innocent. Only in Christ could this take place!

4. What is your natural reaction when Jesus does a dramatic work in the heart of a wicked person? Do you celebrate? Grumble? Doubt? Rejoice? Why?

Jesus told the crowd that Zacchaeus had, in fact, found salvation. And He announced to the crowd that He, the Son of Man, came to seek and save the lost. This is similar to His words in 5:31–32, where Jesus said He came to call sinners (the sick) and not the righteous (the healthy).

5. **Review 19:11–27 and complete the chart below.**

Servant	Return on Investment	Outcome
First		
Second		
Third		

6. Who were the servants? The citizens? The enemies? **Use a study Bible for help.**

Remember, a parable is a story with one main point. Jesus chose to tell this story as He was nearing Jerusalem. He knew His time on earth was coming to an end. This story is significant because Jesus was telling His followers to be good stewards of the wealth (the good news) they'd been given.

The first two servants trusted the character of the nobleman and, therefore, did what he said. They engaged in business and saw a return, and more was entrusted to them. The third servant was disobedient and wrongly accused the nobleman of wickedness. He clearly did not have an accurate view of the nobleman's character. He was corrected and punished for not making more from what he was given. The citizens who hated the nobleman (19:14) were called his enemies when he returned (19:27), and their ultimate punishment was death.

7. If you've been given the good news of Jesus, you've been entrusted with the most valuable thing on earth. How does your view of God shape how you're stewarding what He has given you?

Luke 19:28–48

✝ **READ LUKE 19:28–48**

The exact location of Bethphage is debated among scholars, but many believe it was at the outermost edge of the city of Jerusalem, about half a mile from the city center. Bethany was its own small village nearby—about two miles southeast of Jerusalem. (Note: Mount Olive, Mount Olivet, and the Mount of Olives are all references to the same place.)

1. **Review 19:28–40.**

The two disciples were obedient to Jesus's assignment and went to find the colt He had requested. Pause and consider what these men might have been thinking. Many believed Jesus was going to triumphantly enter the city and overthrow oppressive Roman rule. War heroes don't parade on a baby animal; they mount a mighty horse. Imagine a general turning down a Humvee for an electric scooter. It flies in the face of logic! Jesus's plan for saving humanity was far different from what His followers imagined. He knew He was the Savior sent in fulfillment of Old Testament prophecy (Zechariah 9:9), so He mounted a colt and began His entrance into the city.

2. Look up Matthew's account of this story in Matthew 21:1–10. Use a Bible dictionary and write down the definition of the word *hosanna*.

As Jesus rode into the city, the crowd made a plea for help. They were crying out in adoration to the One they believed would save them. They correctly understood that He was able, but many misunderstood what saving entailed. The Savior came not to free them from political oppression, but to rescue them into a kingdom that would reign forever.

The Pharisees wanted Jesus to silence the crowds, but He said that even if the people present were silent, praise would still abound. Jesus was riding the colt down Mount Olive, which has been covered with gravestones for thousands of years. Estimates say there are as many as 150,000 tombs on that hillside—mostly above ground, with limestone markers. Against this backdrop, it's likely Jesus was using the immediate surroundings in His teaching, as He often did. It's easy to imagine Him gesturing toward the gravestones and basically saying, "Even if the living were to stop praising Me, the souls of the dead would praise Me instead. My praises will exist forever, no matter what."

3. Imagine you were a member of the crowd that day. Write the phrase you would have shouted as Jesus passed by. What are you longing for? How is this longing satisfied in the saving work of Jesus?

4. **Review 19:41–44.**

Next, Jesus came to a place where He overlooked the entire city. And with that view, He wept over the state of Jerusalem. This wasn't the first time Jesus was sorrowful regarding Israel. (Remember 13:6–9, where the gardener caring for the fruitless tree wanted to give it more time to bear fruit?) Jesus was committed to teaching truth, healing the sick, and casting out demons. He was faithful to fertilize the soil and tend to the tree. And when He faced rejection from the religious elite, Jesus was both angry and sorrowful at the hardness of their hearts (Mark 3:5). Jesus, knowing the Scripture, was fully aware of what was in store.

5. **Use a Bible and Bible study tool to complete the chart below.**

Scripture	Prophecy	Fulfillment
Isaiah 6:10		
Micah 3:12		

Keep in mind that the rejection of Jesus confirmed God's plan; it didn't destroy it. And know that the destruction of Jerusalem in AD 70 didn't take God by surprise. He is sovereign over—in control of—every wonderful thing and every difficult thing.

When Jesus arrived at the temple, He was furious enough to weave a whip and start tossing over tables (John 2:15).

6. Fill in the gaps of His declaration in 19:46 (ESV).

"My house shall be a _____ of _____," but you have made it a _____ of _____.

Jesus didn't drive them out because they were selling essential oils or energy drinks in the atrium. He was livid because these merchants were taking advantage of pilgrims who were coming to make offerings by driving up the prices for a sacrificial animal or unjustly adjusting the exchange rates as people needed to convert their monies for an offering. The very place that represented God's generosity in drawing near to mankind was being used to swindle, exploit, and oppress.

As Jesus destroyed the wickedness in the temple, the religious elite could think only of destroying Him. These men had turned a blind eye to the blatant evil in front of them and instead made their focus on ruining the One who came to save them.

Luke 20:1–26

READ LUKE 20:1-26

Yesterday we read that Jesus cleansed the temple, ruffling the feathers of the religious elite. Today, we find Jesus teaching in the temple, sharing the gospel with the crowds, and the frustration of the religious elite is growing.

1. **Review 20:1–8.**

The religious leaders decided to ask Jesus a simple question: "By what authority are You doing these things, or who gave You this authority?" Jesus could've answered their question easily, but He chose to answer with a question of His own.

2. When responding to Jesus's question, what predicament did the religious elite find themselves in?

These highly educated men chose to play dumb. They lied and said they didn't know the answer. If they answered one way, they'd be endorsing Jesus, and if they answered another way, the crowds would be in an uproar. It doesn't seem like Jesus was evading their question, matching trickery for trickery, but rather using a question to explain who He is and perhaps even expose their hypocrisy.

This interruption didn't thwart Jesus's teaching. He continued using His tried-and-true method, the parable, as He shared about wicked tenants.

3. **Review 20:9–18.** Use a Bible study tool to match the characters with the person they represent.

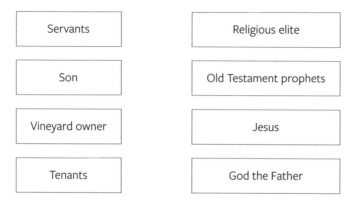

Servants	Religious elite
Son	Old Testament prophets
Vineyard owner	Jesus
Tenants	God the Father

It seems the religious leaders understood Jesus's analogies. When Jesus addressed the wicked tenants' fate, they said, "Surely not!" in disbelief, but Jesus looked directly at them and spoke a passage they all would've known well.

4. **Read Psalm 118:22.** What is a cornerstone? **Use a dictionary for help.** Who is the stone that became a cornerstone?

During the time of Jesus, this passage was known as messianic prophecy, meaning it pointed to the Messiah whom Israel was anticipating. Jesus spoke the language of the religious elite; and by quoting this Scripture, He was essentially saying, "You may reject Me, but I'm the One that everything will be built upon."

5. Revisit 20:18, then read Isaiah 8:14–15 and 1 Peter 2:1–10. What does it mean that many will stumble on the stone? Who are the ones that stumble on the stone?

The message of the gospel—this good news—is foolishness to those who are perishing (1 Corinthians 1:18). People will either rightly place Jesus as the center of their life or they'll stumble, falling away from the only One who can save them.

6. Review 20:19–26.

The religious leaders wanted to lay hands on Jesus—and not in a holy way!—after realizing the magnitude of what He was saying. They wanted to hurt Him, to silence Him, but they were afraid of the people, so they put their heads together and came up with a plan to trick Jesus instead.

7. Summarize 20:21-26 in your own words. What two responses did the religious leaders have to Jesus's words (20:26)?

Jesus's response seemed like a real "mic drop" moment. He saw right through their ulterior motives and into the deep, secret, ugly places they tried to hide. Yet, they failed to look inward and deal with their hardness of heart. The Messiah they were waiting on was right in front of them, and they refused to rightly see Him.

8. When was the last time you marveled at the teachings of Jesus? Write about it in the space below.

Luke 20:27–47

 **READ LUKE 20:27-47**

The religious leaders continued trying to sabotage Jesus and approached Him with a question about the resurrection. Today, we read about the Sadducees, an aristocratic group of religious elite who focused only on the Torah (the first five books of the Old Testament) and followed only the parts they deemed important.

1. **Review 20:27–40.**

2. **Read Deuteronomy 25:5–7.** What instruction is given to the brother of a man who dies and leaves behind a wife?

The brother's role was to protect his brother's line and provide for the woman via an heir. In the Sadducees' hypothetical scenario, if each brother died before having a child with the woman, no brother had special claim to her. Since neither Jesus nor the religious elite could agree that she belonged equally to all seven, the Sadducees believed this scenario disproved the resurrection. But Jesus had a higher viewpoint and responded accordingly.

3. What did Jesus say happens in the next age (afterlife) regarding marriage?

The Sadducees were hoping to disprove the resurrection, but their thoughts on marital relations were tossed out the window as Jesus declared that marriage isn't part of the next age. He spoke to them in their own language again, using another scenario from the second book of the Law (Exodus 3:5–6). In the wilderness of Egypt, God called Himself the God of Abraham, Isaac, and Jacob. He didn't say "I *was* their God," He said, "I *am* their God." Since God is a God of the living, Jesus's evidence of Old Testament language proved to the Sadducees that the resurrection does exist. Imagine these hoity-toity religious men standing before a man from Nazareth with their jaws on the floor!

They were finished asking Him questions, so Jesus asked a difficult question on His own.

4. Fill in the blanks from 20:41.

How can they say that ____ _____ is _____'s _____?

He answers His own question, quoting Psalm 110:1 and pointing out that He is *more* than David's son. This verse is one of the most quoted Old Testament verses in the New Testament. Jesus, Peter, Paul, and the author of Hebrews all used this verse to highlight various aspects of the Messiah.

5. Match the verse with the messianic point highlighted from Psalm 110:1.

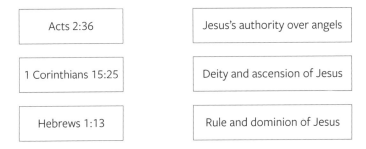

Acts 2:36		Jesus's authority over angels
1 Corinthians 15:25		Deity and ascension of Jesus
Hebrews 1:13		Rule and dominion of Jesus

6. What is the significance of being seated at the right hand of God? What does it mean that His enemies are a footstool? **Use a study Bible and/or read Mark 16:19 (NLT) and Joshua 10:24 for additional help.**

People in His audience understood that the "right hand" was the place of honor and status. Making something your "footstool" meant that your feet were crushing what they were resting on. The Savior has ultimate authority both in heaven and on earth.

7. **Read Revelation 22:16.** What does it mean that Jesus is the root of David? The descendant?

Jesus is both the Creator of David and one who came from the lineage of David. This was spoken by Isaiah (Isaiah 11:1) long before Jesus was born. The religious leaders spent their lives studying Scripture, but continued to be obstinate when the truth of Scripture was before their very eyes. Jesus knew their hearts. The crowds saw their actions. And Jesus gave a strong warning to all those listening.

8. Contrast the behavior of the scribes with the characteristics of a Christ-follower.

In Him there is fullness of life. In Him our strivings cease. When we're fully submitted to the work of the Savior, we don't need to boast like the scribes. We can joyfully surrender all things we hold tightly because we know and believe that He's where the joy is!

9. What stood out to you most in this week's study? Why?

10. What did you learn or relearn about God and His character this week?

Corresponding Psalm & Prayer

 **READ PSALM 81**

1. What correlation do you see between Psalm 81 and this week's study of Jesus as Savior?

2. What portions of this psalm stand out to you most?

3. Close by praying this prayer aloud:

> *Father,*
> *   You are the God of my strength and I praise You. You rescued Your people from slavery and rescued me from the slavery of my*

own sin. Even when I haven't listened to You, You haven't given up on me. You made a way back to Yourself—what mercy! What grace!

Like the Israelites, I've been stubborn and ignored Your voice. And like the people in Jerusalem shouting "Hosanna!" I've wanted my idea of salvation more than I've wanted Your salvation. I've clenched my fists around temporary possessions and turned my back on eternal matters. Like Israel's sin did, my sin has broken Your heart. And I repent.

Increase my faith, Lord. Teach me to pray constantly, with appropriate humility and with righteous confidence in You. Teach me to pray ceaselessly for those who need You. Remind me to pray continually for those who need healing. Prompt me to pray persistently for my faith to increase. And as I pray for my desires, shape my heart to be more like Yours.

I surrender my life to You, Lord—every moment of my day, each decision I make, I yield my will and way to Your perfect will and way.

I love You too. Amen.

Rest, Catch Up, or Dig Deeper

⊥ WEEKLY CHALLENGE

In Luke 18:1–8, Jesus taught about prayer. For some, talking to God is easy, while it's a challenge for others. Throughout Scripture, we see that prayer is vital for the believer. This week, set aside at least twenty minutes to pray in a way that is outside your norm. This could be taking a prayer walk, praying a *lectio divina* style prayer, writing in a prayer journal, getting in a prayer closet, singing your prayer, et cetera. The possibilities are endless, but the challenge this week is to pray in a new way. Minimize your distractions, leave your devices in another room, and lean into growing in this spiritual discipline.

Scripture to Memorize

"He has helped His servant Israel, in remembrance of His mercy . . ."

Luke 1:54

Luke 21–22:
The Preparation of the Savior

DAILY BIBLE READING

Day 1. Luke 21:1–24
Day 2. Luke 21:25–38
Day 3. Luke 22:1–30
Day 4. Luke 22:31–46
Day 5. Luke 22:47–71
Day 6. Psalm 41
Day 7. Catch-Up Day

Corresponds to Days 309 and 314 of *The Bible Recap*.

WEEKLY CHALLENGE

See page 256 for more information.

DAY 1

Luke 21:1–24

 **READ LUKE 21:1-24**

As we draw closer to the last several days of Jesus's life, we'll witness His urgency to communicate the important and difficult truths of the kingdom to His disciples, as well as to the critics whose resistance was escalating.

1. **Review 21:1–4.**

One verse prior to this scene, Jesus warned His disciples that the scribes "devour widows' houses" (20:47), so perhaps this moment was to further contrast the economy of the kingdom and modern religious practices. Jesus saw the rich and He also saw the poor widow, but we know that when Jesus sees something, He sees more than just the actions—He sees the motivations.

2. What do you think their motivations may have been for Jesus to point out this contrast?

Party	Possible Motivation
Rich	
Poor widow	

Scripture references tithes and offerings multiple times, and there are various perspectives on what is right and proper under the new covenant. However, the context of this particular story indicates that its purpose is *descriptive*, not *prescriptive*. In other words, it's a story to illustrate generosity, not a mandate for everyone to give away all their possessions.

The two copper coins, also known as mites, were worth only 1 percent of a daily wage. No one would've minded if she'd decided to give only one of those copper coins and kept the other for herself. But her dependence wasn't on the coins—it was on God's provision. Jesus likely pointed her out to His disciples because she understood the kingdom principle that when God is trusted as the provider of all good things, generosity is always a win-win.

3. Describe a time when you or someone you know gave generously in full dependence on God. What was the outcome?

4. **Review 21:5–9.**

In these next few sections, it could be easy to get bogged down with questions and the fear of the unknown, so be encouraged that Jesus didn't say these things to scare us, but to prepare us. We know fear wasn't His goal because He specifically said, "Do not be terrified" (21:9).

Throughout the Gospels, Jesus assured His followers that persecution and suffering were to be expected in a broken and fallen world. Yet we're often surprised when they happen in our circles today. While Jesus said He is returning soon (Revelation 22:12), sufferings like those in this passage shouldn't spark the assumption of His imminent return. We have been in the "end times" since His ascension two millennia ago, and we will continue to be in the end times until He returns. Some parts of this passage are almost certainly prophesying about the ultimate return of Christ, but it's important to remember that He was talking to His disciples about specific things they would face after His death and resurrection.

While overhearing people talk about the temple adornment, Jesus took the opportunity to confront idolatry. The temple was so revered that to speak against it was considered blasphemy at the same level as denouncing God Himself (Acts 6:11–14). Not only did Jesus explain that the temple would be demolished, but He also warned that many will come claiming to be the Savior. Those who came in Jesus's name likely would come with the political or military might the people were (wrongly) looking for.

5. Why do you think humans are bent toward admiring idols and people above God? How can we keep from being led astray by idols and false representations of Jesus?

6. **Review 21:10–19.** What does 21:13 say about Jesus's intended focus for His disciples in the midst of calamity and persecution? How might this also apply to believers today?

The disciples must've been encouraged when Jesus reassured them of His presence and the promise of wisdom to handle every situation. Not only that, but the instruction not to let their thoughts spin around the "what-ifs" (21:14–17)!

7. Read the verses below and fill in the chart.

Luke 21:19	Philippians 1:6	1 John 2:19
By your endurance you will gain your lives.	I am sure of this, that he who began a good work in you will bring it to completion at the day of Jesus Christ.	They went out from us, but they were not of us; for if they had been of us, they would have continued with us. But they went out, that it might become plain that they all are not of us.

Central Theme:

How might this truth have encouraged the disciples?

8. **Review 21:20–24.**

Here, Jesus continues with a detailed description of coming destruction. But this passage isn't without hope. Jesus assured the disciples that this destruction was "to fulfill all that is written" (21:22). When prophecy is fulfilled, we see evidence of the truths of God's Word.

Some scholars believe 21:24b is not about the fall of Jerusalem to Rome, but that Jesus was painting a larger picture about the news of salvation being brought to the Gentiles around the world. In that interpretation, it is not a time of fear, but a time to delight and rejoice that Jesus is the Savior of all!

Luke 21:25–38

✝ **READ LUKE 21:25-38**

As we continue looking at Jesus's words about the circumstances surrounding His second coming, it's important that we remember His exhortations from yesterday's reading.

1. In the table below, put a check mark next to the truths you most need to remember as we study Christ's return:

	Don't be led astray by leaders who claim to be Jesus but preach a different message. (21:8)
	When the signs feel overwhelming, do not be terrified. (21:9)
	In the suffering, you will have the opportunity to be a witness for the kingdom. (21:13)
	Don't waste time worrying about it. God will give you the exact wisdom you need when you need it. (21:14–15)
	Endurance in suffering leads to eternal blessing. (21:19)
	There is purpose in the pain. (21:22)

2. **Review 21:25–28.**

Though a lot of the imagery in today's passage may seem confusing to the modern reader, it's likely that the first-century readers had a better grasp on what Jesus was describing. These scenes, and the accompanying descriptions in the book of Revelation (chapters 6, 8–9, 15–18), probably aren't meant to be viewed as a multilayered mystery we're trying to solve. After all, *revelation* means "the revealing," not "the concealing."

In many ways, our Christian culture has made the return of Jesus something to be feared, which has caused us to miss the beauty and splendor of God's plan of redemption.

3. **Using a web search, find a reputable source that answers the question *Why did Jesus call Himself the Son of Man?*** Write what you find below. Why would Jesus call Himself the Son of Man when talking about His second coming?

We've briefly discussed the Son of Man earlier in this study (5:24, 12:40, and 19:10). This name is prophesied through the Old Testament as the One who would usher in God's everlasting kingdom. If you've ever experienced the effects of the fall in such a way that left you longing for the kingdom, be encouraged, that's *exactly* what He's talking about!

4. What did Jesus say to do when we begin to see the signs of His return? And why? Is this a new way of thinking about Christ's second coming for you? Why or why not?

5. **Review 21:29–33.** What are some unmistakable signs of changing seasons where you live?

Jesus loved to use the fig tree as an illustration. It seems His intention here was to make the point that just as nature gives signs of season changes, nature will also give a sign of the coming eternal kingdom. Again, this is cause for celebration for those who are in Christ. Do not let anyone cause you to fear the end. Rejoice at the coming redemption of your soul for all of eternity!

6. **Use a concordance or lexicon to look up the word *generation* (21:32).** What are some of the possible meanings?

When we come across something in Scripture that doesn't seem to make sense, it's important to understand the verse not only in the context of the chapter, but in the context of the whole Bible. Jesus Himself said He didn't know the date of His return (Matthew 24:36, Mark 13:32), so He couldn't be saying here that His audience wouldn't die before His return. The best understanding seems to point to "this generation" being the generation of the believers—those who are a part of the new covenant, the church. This is similar to what He said to them in a previous conversation about the Son of Man (Matthew 16:13–20).

The promise is that the church and its confession of the Savior—even in the face of persecution and suffering—would remain until the day of His return. Not only that, but the words of Jesus and the truths of the kingdom would *never* pass away.

7. **Review 21:34–36.** What are we to be careful to avoid? What are we to be careful to do?

We can read this passage with joy and anticipation when we remember Jesus's promise to give us wisdom and words (21:14–15). We don't have to allow our minds to play the "what-if" game when it comes to the return of our Savior.

8. **Review 21:37–38.**

Dr. Luke is intentional about giving his readers context, and these two verses are no exception. In His last days, Jesus was among the people. As He taught in the temple, He was in one of the most crowded places in all of Israel, and He lodged among other travelers who were in town for the Passover. Though He knew the end was coming, Jesus wasn't in hiding. He was on mission, fully engaged with the Father's plan of redemption.

Luke 22:1–30

 READ LUKE 22:1–30

The Jewish festival of Passover was drawing near, and the Jews were preparing to celebrate their ancestors' salvation from Egypt (Exodus 12). If the Passover is a new concept for you, here's a brief overview:

During the last plague against Israel's oppressor, the Lord commanded Moses to instruct each household to kill a spotless lamb at twilight and to (among other things) put its blood on the doorframes of their homes. When the Lord passed through the land of Egypt to strike each firstborn dead, He "passed over" the homes that had been covered in the blood of the spotless lamb and the occupants' lives were saved.

If you're thinking this sounds awfully similar to something that is about to happen in the life of Jesus, you're absolutely right.

1. **Review 22:1–2.** What were the chief priests and scribes doing instead of preparing the people for Passover? What was their motivation?

Fear is never a righteous motivator. If you often find yourself functioning from a place of fear, be encouraged by the message of hope found in our perfect Passover Lamb.

2. Review 22:3–6.

The phrase "Satan entered into Judas" is a tough one to process as believers. To provide helpful context, Judas did nothing against his own will and therefore was responsible for his actions. At the same time, Satan's will was being carried out, as was God's will (Isaiah 53:10). Somehow, all these complex nuances align within God's sovereign plan. Luke probably included this verse to remind his readers that Jesus's ultimate enemy was not man, but Satan. No one twisted Judas's arm—he sought out the religious leaders, agreed to their payment, and joined the conspiracy to see the Savior killed.

3. Why do you think Judas was looking for a time when the crowd was not around?

4. Review 22:7–13.

Following Jesus must have been wild! A simple question from John and Peter led to an answer filled with very specific details that seemed far-fetched. For example, men would not typically be carrying water jars, because in first-century Israel that was a woman's responsibility. Scripture doesn't tell us whether Jesus had prearranged this encounter or He divinely knew what John and Peter would find. Regardless, they'd seen Jesus perform enough miracles to take Him at His word and do what He instructed.

5. When you feel prompted by the Lord, are you more inclined to action or asking questions? Why?

6. **Review 22:14–23.**

As they ate together, Jesus explained each step in the context of what would happen to Him the very next day. All twelve of the disciples were seated at this table, but only one of them knew exactly what Jesus meant when He said, "The hand of him who betrays me is with me on the table."

7. **Read Psalm 41:9–10.** How does it support both God's plan and man's responsibility for sin found in 22:22?

Jesus's words left eleven of the disciples looking at each other and at themselves, attempting to figure out how and who of their inner circle would even consider such betrayal.

8. **Review 22:24–27.** How was this dispute in direct opposition to Jesus's message of the kingdom? What about this conversation is convicting to you?

It's easy to slap our foreheads in shame that the closest men to Jesus missed the point about humility mere hours before His arrest. But put yourselves in their shoes. These men had been taught by Jesus but did not yet have the Holy Spirit. They also had not seen the events of the next several days unfold. Jesus dealt far more kindly with them than we probably would have.

9. **Review 22:28–30.**

Jesus suffered many trials and temptations during His ministry (Hebrews 2:18, 4:15). And while none of His disciples stayed with Him perfectly in all of His trials—especially the trials that still lie ahead in this story—He promised them a few unique blessings. (Note: The exclusion of Judas seems to be a given among scholars.)

10. What three specific blessings are listed in 22:29–30?

11. **Read Revelation 21:14.** What additional blessing is listed here?

It's clear throughout today's reading that there was a specific plan in place for the events that were unfolding. As we continue tomorrow, we'll see even more evidence that God didn't leave the plan of salvation to chance.

Luke 22:31–46

✝ READ LUKE 22:31–46

This section picked up in the middle of the final interactions Luke recorded between Jesus and His disciples prior to His arrest. The guys still didn't seem to fully grasp His message of the kingdom or that He was about to suffer and die. These men were in the midst of a spiritual battle, and while they had the person of Jesus among them, they did not yet have the Holy Spirit within them to help them discern the spiritual reality.

1. **Review 22:31–34.** What did Jesus say Simon Peter would do? What did Simon Peter think he would do?

Satan wanted to destroy the disciples, but Jesus wouldn't allow it. Simon Peter, in his zeal, responded to Jesus with intensity and passion. He may not have *felt* capable of betraying Jesus, but feelings often don't carry us well in trials. Simon Peter's faith would indeed falter.

2. **Review 22:35–38.**

Early in His ministry, Jesus sent His disciples out with nothing, and they were largely received with goodwill (Luke 10:1–17). But here, near the end of His earthly ministry, He gave them different instructions. He told them to use common sense in taking care of themselves. The world they'd encounter without Jesus's presence would be a hostile one.

Jesus's life and ministry fulfilled prophecy after prophecy, and the apostles would've known this better than anyone. So to help His disciples grasp the present reality, He pointed back to a prophecy He was about to fulfill: He would be "numbered with the transgressors." He knew the road ahead would be full of suffering for the men in the room with Him, and in His final hours, He aimed to prepare them well.

3. Have you ever sincerely thought about the cost of following Jesus, knowing that you would face suffering? Why did you find it worth it?

When Jesus mentioned swords during His instructions, the disciples took an inventory of their weapons. Among the group, they had two swords, and Jesus told them that it was enough. Scholars have various views on what He meant by this. Some believe He was saying, "That's enough swords for the journey ahead." Others think He was saying, "That's enough of this conversation." Still others believe His request for swords was in preparation for His arrest—after all, since He was going to be accused of insurrection, there had to be "evidence" among His followers that He was a threat.

4. **Read 22:39–46.**

Jesus needed to pray. Luke tells his readers that this was Jesus's custom. His relationship with and dependence on the Father was a primary marker of His life.

5. Why do you think Jesus links prayer and temptation in His instructions to the disciples? How do they link in your life?

Jesus's prayer was one of sheer desperation. His flesh wanted nothing to do with the series of events He knew was coming, *and yet* He was willing to surrender to the Father's plan. To be clear, the will of the Father was also the will of the Son and the Spirit. The triune God does everything in unity within Himself, and it was His plan of salvation from before the foundation of the world (Revelation 13:8).

The agony of the physical, human reality Jesus would face was enough to require heavenly intervention and strength. Even with this support, Luke tells us that Jesus's sweat appeared like drops of blood. Scholars differ on whether Luke meant the volume of liquid coming out of Jesus's body or that His sweat was so great that His capillaries opened and blood mixed with His sweat (a condition known as hematohidrosis). Either way, there was visible evidence of Jesus's internal agony.

6. Why were the disciples asleep instead of praying? Have you ever been tempted to shut down instead of engaging emotionally with something God asked you to lean into? If so, briefly describe the situation.

Perhaps they were tired from a meal of only bread and wine. Or perhaps it felt easier to disconnect from what was happening rather than face it head on. Jesus had told the disciples one would betray Him, He was going to die, and they would face suffering. He implored them to stay awake to the spiritual realities and engage with the solution to victory: prayer.

Be encouraged that because of the incredible work of our Savior on the cross, we have the power of the Holy Spirit dwelling in us, giving us direct access to the Father's wisdom, strength, and discernment. Prayer is always a source of strength for us when we face battles!

Luke 22:47–71

 **READ LUKE 22:47–71**

1. **Review 22:47–53.**

Jesus was mid-conversation with at least eleven of His disciples when a crowd approached, led by the twelfth, Judas. And they had hardened hearts and malicious minds.

2. What did a kiss signify in first-century Israel? **Do a web search or use a commentary for help.** How did Judas's use of a kiss magnify the sting of betrayal?

Surely feeling the sting of Judas's betrayal himself, Simon Peter recognized what was about to happen and drew one of their two swords (John 18:10).

He had told Jesus he was prepared to die, and he seemed ready to display that intention.

3. How did Jesus respond to Simon Peter's actions? Why do you think He did this?

Jesus had a singular mission in mind; violence and resistance were not on the agenda. After performing a miracle in front of everyone, He turned His attention to the religious elite of the crowd. Neither Jesus's miracles nor His message would be received by these men whose minds were already made up.

4. What was Jesus's accusation of the religious leaders? What do you think He meant?

5. **Review 22:54–62.**

Stepping away from the story of Jesus for a moment, Luke zoomed in on Simon Peter, giving an incomplete timeline of what happened to Jesus on that night. For a fuller picture, read this story in the other gospels. It seems Luke wanted to focus on Simon Peter's story for a reason.

When Jesus was seized, Simon Peter followed from a distance, then sat down by the fire, among people who had been a part of Jesus's arrest. It seemed he wanted to stay close enough to know what was happening, but far enough to disassociate himself from Jesus.

6. Fill in the chart below according to 22:56–60. What were the accusations leveled against Simon Peter, and how did he respond to each?

Accusation	Simon Peter's Response

7. Have you ever been in a situation where distancing yourself from Jesus felt necessary for self-preservation? How did you feel afterward?

Before he could get the words of denial out of his mouth, the sound of the rooster's crow snapped Simon Peter back to his senses. He'd been so concerned with self-preservation that he'd completely forgotten what Jesus had said only hours before. At that very moment, Jesus was in the courtyard and made eye contact with him. This scene is heartbreaking.

This look from Jesus didn't seem to be one of condemnation, but between the sound of the rooster and the recognition of his guilt, Simon Peter was crushed. The bitter weeping was the sign of a man dealing with his sin in a way that would lead him to restoration rather than ruin.

8. **Review 22:63–65.** List the actions that led to each of the types of pain that were inflicted on Jesus:

Emotional:

Physical:

Spiritual:

How can knowing that Jesus experienced each of these types of pain be an encouragement to you in your own pain?

9. **Review 22:66–71.**

Luke didn't tell us about the illegal midnight trial, but suffice it to say, this trial seems like an attempt to save face and "make it legal," even though there were plenty of things about this trial that went against Jewish laws and customs.

The line of questioning from the religious leaders revealed that their only purpose was to uphold their conclusions, not to ensure justice was served. Jesus answered them with one of the most condemning statements in all of Scripture, "If I tell you, you will not believe." Jesus had told them the answer many times, yet they didn't believe Him. He went on to tell them what would happen, and they saw it as justification rather than a conviction of their own hearts.

10. What was their response to Jesus as the promised Savior? What does this tell you about their hearts? Do you ever find yourself trying to spiritually justify your own conclusions rather than sincerely seeking righteousness in God's Word?

The religious elite had all the evidence they needed to believe Him. He'd fulfilled prophecy after prophecy, He'd performed miracles, He'd cared for the marginalized. Yet the religious leaders were too stuck in their own rituals to see clearly. Though their hardness of heart is gut-wrenching to read, we know God used their callous, sinful actions for His own glory. We know what happens at the end of the story, and it confirms that He's where the joy is!

11. What stood out to you most in this week's study? Why?

12. What did you learn or relearn about God and His character this week?

DAY 6

Corresponding Psalm & Prayer

 **READ PSALM 41**

1. What correlation do you see between Psalm 41 and this week's study of Jesus as Savior?

2. What portions of this psalm stand out to you most?

3. Close by praying this prayer aloud:

Father,
*   I praise You because You are sovereign over all things. You sent*
Your Son to fulfill the prophets, to face His transgressors, to die as

the Passover Lamb, and to provide a way to You forever. Even the worst sin won't stop You. I praise You for Your sovereign plan!

Be gracious to me—I have sinned against You. While You gave everything, I've hoarded my cheap copper coins. Though I've eaten Your bread, I've still denied You—sometimes with my words and sometimes with my actions. I've doubted You in times of suffering, and I've hid from situations where I could've been a witness for You. Fear of man has been my motivation at times, instead of a righteous fear of You. And I repent.

Deepen my faith, and help me to show integrity even in the face of suffering and persecution. Remind me of Your promise that even though hard times will come, You'll be with me. Help me believe to my core that You are all I need, no matter what comes my way.

I surrender my life to You, Lord—every moment of my day, each decision I make, I yield my will and way to Your perfect will and way.

I love You too. Amen.

Rest, Catch Up, or Dig Deeper

✝ WEEKLY CHALLENGE

All four gospel accounts give various snapshots of the arrest, abuses, trials, and crucifixion of Jesus. Having a complete picture helps make it real. Using all four gospels and online Bible study tools, write out the order of events from Christ's arrest to His crucifixion. If scholars disagree about some details of the timeline, that's okay—this isn't graded! The point of this practice isn't only to accumulate information, but to accumulate awe and gratitude. As you take an extended, detailed look at what Jesus went through, let His experience fill your heart with gratitude for your Savior and His salvation.

— Scripture to Memorize —

" . . . as He spoke to our
fathers, to Abraham and
to His offspring forever."

Luke 1:55

Luke 23–24:

Salvation through the Savior

DAILY BIBLE READING

Day 1. Luke 23:1–25

Day 2. Luke 23:26–43

Day 3. Luke 23:44–56

Day 4. Luke 24:1–35

Day 5. Luke 24:36–53

Day 6. Psalm 134

Day 7. Catch-Up Day

Corresponds to Days 317 and 319 of *The Bible Recap*.

WEEKLY CHALLENGE

See page 282 for more information.

Luke 23:1–25

 **READ LUKE 23:1-25**

Today we walk with Jesus through His accusation, trial, and verdict.

1. **Review 23:1–5.** Fill in the blanks of the three accusations against Jesus.

_____ the nation.

_____ _____ to give _____ to Caesar.

_____ that He is Christ, _____ _____.

Rome was always on guard against insurrection. The Zealots garnered quite a reputation as a fanatical sect of Jews intent on leading a revolt against Rome. And here was the Sanhedrin, the leading council of the Jews, building a case that Jesus was the exact type of insurrectionist they feared most.

As for their third accusation, Jesus certainly claimed to be king, but He was clear He had no intention of being a political one (John 18:36–37). Their second accusation is proved false in 20:20–26, because He had specifically said to give Caesar what was his.

Nevertheless, only Pilate had the power to enact capital punishment, so the Sanhedrin had to create political propaganda to support their agenda. Regardless of what it took, Jesus must go.

2. **Review 23:6–16.** The trial continued in 23:6–12 as Herod weighed in. Match the leading authorities with their reason for rejecting Jesus.

Sanhedrin	Refusal to take Jesus seriously.
Pilate	Jealousy and fear of losing control.
Herod	Unwilling to take a stand against the crowd.

The Sanhedrin had been wary and jealous of Jesus from the beginning. He was a threat to their power, and they refused to lose it.

Pilate wasn't a religious leader, though; he was a political figurehead who didn't see Jesus as much of a threat. But a crowd can be a powerful thing, and he succumbed to their cries. Compromise always seems like a good solution when you take a crowd more seriously than a king.

Herod was intrigued by Jesus, but when Jesus refused to impress him, he reverted to sarcasm and cynicism. Herod wasn't interested in a Savior; he wanted a performer.

3. These rejections of Jesus are still common today. How do you see these three reactions active on the earth? How do you see them active in your own heart? Take your time. Be honest.

Reaction	Evidence on the earth	Evidence in your own heart
Fear and jealousy		
Compromise to a crowd		
Sarcasm and cynicism		

Please note: Many translations exclude 23:17, because this sentence appears to have been added to an early version of Luke's letter. However, the content is recorded in other gospels (Matthew 27:15 and Mark 15:6).

4. **Review 23:18–25. Using your favorite Bible dictionary, look up Barabbas.** What does his name mean? What is the significance of Jesus taking his place?

This was a disturbing and sobering scene. Picture a Roman oppressor standing in front of an oppressed crowd attempting to defend a small-town, miracle-working teacher. The hatred was probably palpable. But none of this angst and anger was pointed at the one oppressing them; instead, it was directed at the One sent to free them. Perhaps some of these people had cried out "Hosanna" just days before, but here their voices joined in a different cry: "Give us Barabbas and crucify Jesus!" It was customary for the governor to release a prisoner during the Feast of Passover (Matthew 27:15–18), so Pilate relented.

This is a brutal and beautiful picture of what Jesus was about to do for all of humanity. The jail cell meant for a murderer would now hold the mender of hearts. The verdict spoken over a man worthy of death was now spoken over the Man worthy of praise. The cross meant to be carried by a criminal was placed on the shoulders of a spotless lamb.

Barabbas was a picture of us all. Barabbas literally translates to "son of the father." Here, the Son of God took the place of the children of wrath (Ephesians 2:3). For every one of us has sinned and fallen short of the glory of God (Romans 3:23). The wages of that sin is death (Romans 6:23). Jesus stepped in and took the death we deserved. We are the voices crying out in the crowd. We are the criminals being set free.

5. According to 23:25, whose will did Pilate hand Jesus over to?

6. Match the Scripture reference with its text:

Isaiah 53:10	"They are the ones whose names were not written in the Book of Life that belongs to the Lamb who was slaughtered before the world was made."
John 10:18	"No one takes it from me, but I lay it down of my own accord."
Revelation 13:8 (NLT)	"Yet it was the will of the Lord to crush him."

Before we point fingers of accusation at this crowd or an entire people group, let us remember that our God is in control, always and forever sovereign in will and direction. Jesus was not at the mercy of Pilate or the people. Father, Son, and Spirit had been operating in complete unity since the foundation of the world in this perfect plan of redemption. And this is good news! As tragic as the solution to our sin problem was, we *needed* Him to die; every person and regime participating in that process was a necessary part of the redemption story. He was crushed for our iniquities, and with His wounds we are healed.

Luke 23:26–43

READ LUKE 23:26-43

Today we gather around the cross of Jesus Christ. And we do not gather there alone.

1. **Skim through the entire passage again and write down every individual or group of people mentioned other than Jesus.**

This crucifixion account held a unique and beautiful perspective that we can easily miss if we read it too quickly. Luke, our detailed scribe, spends little to no time recording the details of the crucifixion itself. There is no mention of Jesus's body being beaten beyond recognition. No sign of the crown of thorns. No description of the nails being hammered into Christ's flesh. No sight of the spear. Could it be that Dr. Luke, educated on the medical effects of such torture on a human body, could not bring himself to pen his Savior's pain? Certainly, he had heard every brutal detail about the murder scene from numerous eyewitnesses. Yet he focused only on what Jesus seemed to be most focused on—the crowd around the cross.

2. **Review 23:26.**

We aren't given many details about Simon. We know that he was from Cyrene (a city located in modern-day Libya). He had already traveled some eight hundred miles, likely for the Feast of Passover. But there was still quite a journey for him to walk. Luke clearly informed us that Simon carried Jesus's cross (likely just the crossbeam) *behind* Him. Simon followed in Jesus's actual footsteps with a beam on his back as a physical representation of what Christ now invites every disciple to do (Luke 9:23, 14:27). Simon knew he wouldn't have to face eternal death on the cross he carried. And now, because of Jesus, neither do we.

3. **Review 23:27–31.** This encounter is recorded only in Luke's gospel. What do you think: Who were the "daughters of Jerusalem"? What was the meaning of the green and dry wood?

Jesus was likely followed by a group of women who sought to give condemned men a drugged drink as a means of relief. Jesus received nothing but offered a warning. He had already given multiple warnings about the danger of rejecting Him and of the coming destruction (19:43; 21:6, 21:22–24). And on the path to His own death, His heart turned toward His people. He even warned them again, "If this is the fate of the green wood [Jesus referring to His own innocence], what will happen to the dry wood [those who are guilty and worthy of punishment]?" These were not easy words, but it is the lavish love of Christ that called people to repentance even as He walked toward death.

4. **Review 23:32–38.** Write down Jesus's prayer in 23:34. What does this mean for the crowd? What does this mean for us?

It's vital for us to imagine this scene so the gravitas of this prayer doesn't fade like a whisper into the crowd. The cross is not easy to look at, but we *must* look at it. In it lies our salvation.

Imagine His eyes bruised and swollen shut from beatings.
Imagine His lungs collapsing and filling with fluid.
Imagine ragged splinters digging into His raw and exposed spine.
Imagine the physical torment.
Imagine the loneliness and psychiatric strain.

Now imagine a pain greater than that pain, an ache that made all other pain bearable, even worth it: the ache of God separated from His sinful people, longing for restoration. Imagine a God so kind, so compassionate, so devoted to fulfill His eternal plan and restore unity with His beloved people that He endured unthinkable scourging, accepted blatant and belittling verbal abuse, and received the body-shaking sting of cold metal in His flesh. And still, He blinked through blurred vision to look at the rulers and soldiers who willed it all and prayed, "Father, forgive them."

This is the God who prayed over them. This is the God who prays over us.

5. Pause and just thank Jesus. Do not hurry past this moment. These are holy things we are called to remember (22:19).

6. **Review 23:39–43.** What were the two criminals' reactions to Jesus? What was the result?

	Reaction to Jesus	Result
Criminal #1		
Criminal #2		

We don't know the moment when one criminal's heart turned toward repentance. Perhaps he had heard Jesus pray over their executioners and hoped that same grace could extend even to him. What we do know is that God's kindness leads to repentance (Romans 2:4). And no one got a perspective of God's kindness quite like this man who hung at His side as He forgave His crucifers.

It's never too late for God to save. Look back to page 153 and write down, again, the names of the five or more people you're still praying would receive Jesus as their Lord and Savior. Spend some time praying for them.

Luke 23:44–56

READ LUKE 23:44-56

1. **Review 23:44–49.** Mark the times mentioned in 23:44–45.

In the middle of the day when the sun is meant to be at its highest point, the earth went dark from 12:00–3:00 p.m. Why? God used physical events to represent supernatural realities.

In the beginning, God spoke a creative word *and* a prophetic word, "Let there be light" (Genesis 1:1). In John 1:1–4, the apostle picked up this prophetic cry, "In the beginning was the Word . . . in him was the life, and the life was the light of men." Jesus *was* and *is* the Light of life. The light of day faded as the Light of men died. But we know the darkness does not overcome Him (John 1:5)!

As He died, another spiritual reality was ripping into the natural as the veil of the temple was torn in two. No longer would God be shrouded behind thick curtains, where only a righteous few could enter. All could now approach the presence of God with confidence (Hebrews 4:16).

2. Write down Jesus's final prayer on the cross from 23:46.

Jesus is eternally God, but was also fully man. In His time on earth, He continually submitted His flesh to His divinity. The *Spirit* led Him into the wilderness to be tempted (4:1). He returned to Galilee in the strength of the *Spirit* (4:14). He says in John 5:19 that "the Son can do nothing of his own accord, but only what he sees the Father doing." Hebrews 5:7–10 even says He had to learn obedience, much of it through prayer. This was evident in the final hours before His betrayal when He prayed, "Not my will, but yours, be done" (Luke 22:42). Unceasing communion with the Father and the Spirit had empowered His life, and now it would empower His death.

3. Jesus lived wholly submitted in all areas of His life, including His death. Consider the chart below, and take some time to ask God where you are most trying to live in your own strength. Circle two to three areas. Seeking the guidance of the Holy Spirit, write at least one action step for each area you circled that will physically represent your spiritual reliance.

Area of Life	Action Step
Finances	
Relationships	
Physical health	

Area of Life	Action Step
Career/job	
Hobbies/ recreation	

4. What was the centurion's first response to Jesus's death?

When Jesus breathed His last, the centurion declared Jesus innocent while also praising God. Such a strange response to the realization that you'd assisted in beating, humiliating, and murdering an innocent man! It seems as if all these physical events worked together to convince him of the supernatural reality. Maybe he'd heard Jesus's prayers. Maybe he'd heard Jesus's interaction with the criminal. Maybe the sky falling dark in the middle of it all had enlightened his spiritual eyes. Something about the way Jesus died convinced the centurion of His identity. Let that sink in.

5. God can use dark circumstances to illuminate spiritual truths. How has God used the pain of others or even your own suffering to reveal Himself to you? Consider sharing this story with a friend or family member, praising God with your testimony.

6. **Review 23:50–56.** Let's do another quick social media profile! Write down every detail about Joseph in 23:50–53.

We know from Luke's and John's gospels that Joseph was a secret follower of Jesus who held a high-ranking position in the Sanhedrin. This means he'd likely been in many (if not all) of the conversations surrounding Jesus's trial and verdict. We know he disapproved, but we don't know whether he spoke up. Joseph may not have served Jesus in many ways, but at His death, he served the Savior in a way that only he could. None of Jesus's poor apostles could've afforded a way to get Christ's body off the cross or provide a tomb for Him.

7. **Revisit 23:54–56 and read Exodus 12:21–28. Using a Bible dictionary or encyclopedia, look up "day of Preparation."** What is the significance of Jesus dying on this day?

A sacrificial lamb was the focus of the Passover meal. In the four days leading up to the feast, every family would select a *perfect* lamb. On the day before Passover, the day of Preparation, they would sacrifice it, place its blood over the doorways of their homes, and then eat the lamb together at sundown. This meal, this sacrifice, was done every year in remembrance of God delivering them from slavery in Egypt. The blood of the lamb had covered them from judgment and made a way for them to walk toward the land of promise.

It was made clear in 23:54–56: Jesus is now the perfect Passover Lamb. His blood made a way for the judgment of sin to pass over us. His sacrifice provides the path to true freedom.

Our passage concludes with women going to prepare spices and ointments to later embalm Jesus's mutilated body. Their day ended in grief and darkness. We will end there, as well. Let the weight of Jesus's sacrifice work in your heart before you move to the rest of your day.

Luke 24:1–35

 **READ LUKE 24:1-35**

Who's ready for a day full of good news?

1. **Review 24:1–7.**

If you have a favorite true crime podcast or show, you know what a vital role evidence plays in an investigation. *The greater the evidence, the greater the argument.* Whether it's used to convict, defend, or rectify—evidence plays a crucial role in the certainty of a claim.

When it came to the miraculous claim that a man rose from the dead when an entire city had seen Him crucified just days earlier, Luke needed to record substantial evidence to validate the testimony of the empty tomb:

- A stone was rolled away.
- No dead body was found.
- Men dressed in dazzling clothes (angels) confirmed He had risen.
- At least four people saw the tomb empty.
- The linen burial cloths were left behind.

- And if that wasn't enough, there's the fact that Jesus Himself had testified repeatedly that this would happen (Luke 9:22, 9:44, 18:31–33).

There have been much less significant cases won by much less evidence. Luke is no second-rate investigator either. In his book *The Bearing of Recent Discovery on the Trustworthiness of the New Testament*, Sir William Ramsay, who was an archaeologist and leading authority on the history of Asia Minor, wrote, "[I take] the view that Luke's history is unsurpassed in its trustworthiness. . . . You may press the words of Luke in a degree beyond any other historian's, and they will stand the keenest scrutiny and the hardest treatment."[*]

Let the verdict of the dazzling angels stand: "He is not here, but has risen."

2. **Review 24:8–12.** Who was at the tomb early that morning? Why were they there?

The women we read about in 23:55–56 were probably the same women mentioned here. According to Jewish law, men weren't allowed to touch dead bodies because it made them ceremonially unclean. Culture had assigned women this lowly job of embalming a body. But at the empty tomb, we see the life of Jesus already creating a new kingdom. Though they had come to the tomb carrying spices to anoint a body, they left the tomb anointed to carry the gospel message. The world may have overlooked women, even belittled them. But Jesus entrusted women with the message and empowered them to go and share the good news!

Peter received this news from the women and ran to see for himself. Sure enough, Jesus was not there. So where was He?

---

[*] Sir William M. Ramsay, *The Bearing of Recent Discovery on the Trustworthiness of the New Testament*, 4th ed. (London: Hodder and Stoughton, 1920), 81, 89.

3. **Review 24:13–27.** Let's practice a little geography! Circle Jerusalem on the map below. Then circle Emmaus* and draw a line between them representing a road.

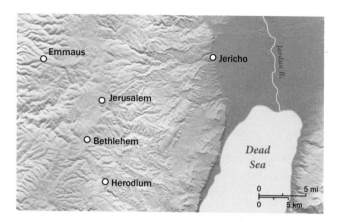

Luke moved from the evidence of an empty tomb to the eyewitness accounts of Jesus seen alive!

4. Fill in the blanks to complete 24:15.

While they were talking and discussing together, Jesus himself _____ _____ and _____ _____ _____.

This one verse could be a theological statement describing new life in the kingdom. It's no accident that this is what Jesus did right after He rose from the dead. It's a small story that reveals the wider narrative. Because of His sacrifice, death, and resurrection, humanity does not have to go to a *place* to encounter the presence of God. No temple needed. No more sacrifices required. The Spirit of Jesus now fills every believer and joins them on every journey, progressively revealing the Savior so that we may become more like Him (John 15:26).

---

* Experts disagree on the exact location of Emmaus.

5. Match the Old Testament prophecy to its New Testament fulfillment.

Genesis 12:3	Luke 4:28–29
Isaiah 7:14	Matthew 2:14–15
Hosea 11:1	Acts 3:25–26
Isaiah 53:3	Luke 1:35

There are over 400 messianic prophecies recorded in the Old Testament. You just did an exercise to show how Jesus fulfilled four of them. In actuality, He fulfilled nearly *350* to the absolute letter during His earthly ministry (the others pertain to the future).

To put this in perspective, the mathematical probability of one person fulfilling just *eight* prophecies perfectly is 1 in 10^{17} (100,000,000,000,000,000). The probability of one person fulfilling sixteen prophecies is 1 in 10^{45} (1,000,000,000,000,000,000,000,000,000,000,000,000,000,000,000). These figures are from a study conducted by Professor Peter Stoner at Westmont College, verified by the American Scientific Affiliation and documented in his book *Science Speaks*.*

For one man to perfectly fulfill nearly 350 prophecies is an unbelievable mathematical improbability. (If you want additional algebraic assistance on this specific equation you'll have to buy another book. This is a Bible study. Just know this is a math only the Bible could create. Bible math!)

In this moment, Jesus took the entirety of Scripture and pointed it to Himself. This is amazing, and this is the Savior.

6. **Review 24:28–35.** When did the travelers realize that the man traveling with them was Jesus? What's the significance of *how* their eyes were opened?

* Peter W. Stoner, *Science Speaks: An Evaluation of Certain Christian Evidences* (Chicago: Moody Press, 1963), 106, 108.

Even after their Emmaus walk and seminary class, the men still didn't recognize Jesus. Not until He broke bread with them.

This was a physically and spiritually eye-opening moment. Imagine Jesus sitting down at the table, breaking the bread, and handing it to each of them. Perhaps it was at this moment, as He stretched out His arm to hand them the bread, that they saw His wrists for the first time, still carrying the scars of crucifixion. As they did, their eyes were opened and they truly saw. The new covenant Jesus had instituted around a dinner table just a few nights before was now offered in full: "This is my body, which is given for you" (22:19).

Jesus was alive! As they lifted their eyes in this awe-filled realization, He was gone. But don't worry, they see Him again tomorrow.

Luke 24:36–53

 **READ LUKE 24:36–53**

Today starts with a jump scare!

1. **Review 24:36–37.**

The disciples in a locked room: "We saw Jesus on the road! He's alive!"
Jesus, appearing out of nowhere: "Is somebody talking about Me?"

Whether Jesus did this as a further revelation of His deity or a display of His sense of humor (or both), certainly we'd respond like the disciples did.

2. **Review 24:38–43.** What did Jesus do to convince the disciples it was really Him and not a spirit? What does this reveal about His humanity and His divinity?

One of Luke's main agendas is to reveal Jesus as the Son of Man. As a matter of fact, Son of Man is the title Jesus most uses in reference to Himself.

3. All of Luke's references are listed below. Count them and write down the total as a means of grasping just how important this is. Circle five of them and look them up to refresh your memory on these stories we've covered.

5:24	9:58	17:26	22:22
6:5	11:30	17:30	22:48
6:22	12:8	18:8	22:69
7:34	12:10	18:31	24:7
9:22	12:40	19:10	
9:26	17:22	21:27	
9:44	17:24	21:36	

Total: _____

All these references were spoken by Jesus Himself, except for the last one—which was spoken by the angel who was quoting Jesus when announcing His resurrection.

In Genesis 1–2, God created humanity to rule the earth *with* Him. But humanity chose sin and broke this divine partnership. God punished Adam and Eve, but also gave them a promise—a child would be born to reinstitute God's perfect kingdom (Genesis 3:15). Centuries later, a Jewish exile named Daniel received a prophetic dream that referred to this Savior as "the Son of Man." For humanity to be saved, a perfect human would come, defeat the power of sin and death, and establish an everlasting kingdom (Daniel 7:13–14).

If Jesus really was the Savior, it was imperative that He came as a human, died as a human, and was raised as a human. This is why He invited the disciples to see His *physical* scars and touch His *physical* body. This small act revealed a salvific truth: *"I am the Son of Man—the Savior of the world."*

And if that weren't enough, He asked for some food. Ghosts don't eat, but humans do (preferably not *broiled* fish, but we'll cut the disciples some slack considering they were in hiding).

4. Review 24:44–45. Flip back to yesterday's study as an aid to fill in the blanks.

Number of Old Testament messianic prophecies: _____

Number of messianic prophecies Jesus fulfilled during His earthly ministry:

_____

The disciples had grown up being trained in every letter of the law. They could quote the messianic prophecies. Their entire Jewish calendar was oriented around remembering the work of God and living in hopeful expectation of the Messiah. And still, they needed help to see Jesus as the fulfillment of it all.

Familiarity and education aren't enough to truly see the spiritual significance held in a book that is living and active. Scriptural revelation always requires God's help. Thank God for the Holy Spirit, our Helper.

5. If you've gone through this entire Bible study and still feel like there's so much you don't understand, *take heart!* This walk with Jesus is a life-long journey. Spend some time writing a prayer, casting all your biblical insecurities on God. Ask for more wisdom and more of the Holy Spirit's help. Jesus promises to answer those requests with a yes (Luke 11:13, James 1:5).

6. Review 24:46–49 and rejoice! The gospel was on its way to us.

This is Luke's account of the Great Commission (see also Matthew 28:16–20). The bottom line? The disciples were to go and make more disciples out of *all nations*. Jesus sent them out with the power of the Holy Spirit to the ends of the earth—*that's us*!

Whether you're reading this with a group in South Carolina or by yourself in Singapore, you are proof that Jesus's commission is being fulfilled. The message of Jesus's resurrection was carried from that small room, by a handful of people, across centuries and seas, to make its way to you. Glory to God!

7. **Review 24:50–53.** Where does Luke's account end?

Luke's gospel started with Zechariah serving in the temple and ended with the disciples rejoicing in the temple. Luke's gospel is quite literally wrapped in the joy of Jesus and His presence.

As we close the book on this study, let's leave the same way Luke left the disciples—rejoicing together with one voice that He's where the joy is!

8. What stood out to you most in this week's study? Why?

9. What did you learn or relearn about God and His character this week?

DAY 6

Corresponding
Psalm & Prayer

READ PSALM 134

1. What correlation do you see between Psalm 134 and this week's study of Jesus as Savior?

2. What portions of this psalm stand out to you most?

3. Close by praying this prayer aloud:

Father,
Your Son's blood marked my life so that the judgment of sin passed over me. You defeated death and the grave and made a way

for me to be with You forever. What joy! I join with all the saints who have gone before me—all those in Your family who have already passed through the curtain of death—and with all the saints alive today and all those who will come after me as we bless Your name. You alone are the true, eternal God!

Yet even as I've seen Your miraculous work, I've still kept certain areas of my life separate from You, not submitting them or myself to Your perfect plan. When troubles have come my way, I've pointed my finger at You instead of at our fallen, broken world or my own sinful actions.

I am Barabbas, the sinful prisoner set free because of Your perfect sacrifice. And when You took my place, You prayed over me. Your love is breathtaking—it is both heartbreaking and heart restoring.

I want to understand You and Your kingdom more. Multiply my efforts and send Your Spirit to give me wisdom, so that day after day, I will learn more about who You are and what You're doing and how much You love Your kids.

I surrender my life to You, Lord—every moment of my day, each decision I make, I yield my will and way to Your perfect will and way.

I long for Your return. Come soon. And until then, may You find me rejoicing.

I love You too. Amen.

DAY 7

Rest, Catch Up, or Dig Deeper

✝ WEEKLY CHALLENGE

We complete our study this week with Jesus's death, burial, and resurrection. As we do, let's look back over the past ten weeks and remember all He walked through in His journey to the cross.

Go back through each week of this study and write down a way you were impacted or a moment when God and His Word spoke to you. If you're feeling creative, make an art piece documenting what you've learned in each chapter of this study.

God is continuing to teach you more about Himself and grow you in intimacy with Him. Praise Him for what He has done in you already. Let this reflection also guide you into what you're still asking God to do in your life. Remember—the cross, burial, and resurrection of Jesus Christ mean there is always hope!

FOR GROUP LEADERS

Thank you for using this study and leading others through it as well! Each week has a wide variety of content (content and questions, daily Bible reading, Scripture memorization, weekly challenge, and resources) to help the reader develop a range of spiritual disciplines. Feel free to include as much or as little of that in your meetings as you'd like. The details provided in How to Use This Study (pp. 11–13) will be helpful to you and all your group members, so be sure to review that information together!

It's up to you and your group how you'd like to structure your meetings, but we suggest including time for discussion of the week's study and Bible text, mutual encouragement, and prayer. You may also want to practice your Scripture memory verses together as a group or in pairs. As you share with each other, "consider how to stir up one another to love and good works" (Hebrews 10:24) and "encourage one another and build one another up" (1 Thessalonians 5:11).

Here are some sample questions to help facilitate discussion. This is structured as a weekly study, but if your group meets at a different frequency, you may wish to adjust the questions accordingly. Cover as many questions as time allows, or feel free to come up with your own. And don't forget to check out the additional resources we've linked for you at MyDGroup.org/Resources/Luke.

Sample Discussion Questions

What questions did this week's study or Bible text bring up for you?

What stood out to you in this week's study?

What did you notice about God and His character?

How were you challenged by your study of the Bible text? Is there anything you want to change in light of what you learned?

How does what you learned about God affect the way you live in community?

What correlation did you see between the psalm from Day 6 and this week's study of Jesus as Savior?

Have you felt God working in you through the weekly challenge? If so, how?

Is your love for God's Word increasing as we go through this study? If so, how?

Did anything you learned increase your joy in knowing Jesus?

ACKNOWLEDGMENTS

Olivia Le, who makes all our writing summits run smoothly—from flights to food to fun times!

Rachel Mantooth, who breathed life into us along the way.

Laura Buchelt, who built out a great structure for us and serves as our head cheerleader.

Emily Pickell, who is steady and unflappable, always bringing beautiful insights and wisdom.

Meredith Knox, who provided awe-inducing content *and* comic relief.

Meg Mitchell, Evaline Asmah, and Brittney Flagg, who made it all work seamlessly from afar.

Lisa Jackson, Jeff Braun, and Hannah Ahlfield, who help keep us from stumbling as we move at this rapid pace.